Your Life.
Your Way.
ReDefined.

Combining Psychology & Creativity for Successful Life Transitions

Barbara McFarland, EdD, and
Alta Bradford

authorHOUSE®

1663 Liberty Drive
Bloomington, IN 47403
www.authorhouse.com
Phone: 1-800-839-8640

First published by AuthorHouse 7/9/2010

ISBN: 978-1-4520-4489-7 (e)
ISBN: 978-1-4520-4488-0 (sc)

Library of Congress Control Number: 2010909271

Printed in the United States of America
Bloomington, Indiana

This book is printed on acid-free paper.

Contents

Acknowledgments

As a way to test our model and its viability, we conducted a pilot session and would like to thank the following women for giving us their time and valuable feedback:

- Susan D. Stewart
- Suzanne Brown
- Jennifer Mayhall
- Deborah Fuller
- Mar Feder
- Marlene Bubash
- Colleen K. Foegle
- Renee Adams

Much gratitude goes to Jan Hamilton for being completely unflappable and tremendously resilient through many rounds of changes in layout and copy. We could not have done it without you.

Many, many thanks go to Dean Varner for his amazing ability to proof and edit multiple versions of our manuscript and still maintain an eagle eye for detail and a sharp ear for consistency.

"The foolish man seeks happiness in the distance. The wise grows it under his feet." – **James Oppenheim**

Introduction

This book is about redefining yourself – using life transitions as
the catalyst for change. It explores a model that blends positive
psychology and creativity to give you a framework that identifies
how you can be the person you have dreamed about being
– about having the kind of future you have longed to have.

As a brand design strategist (Alta) and a psychologist (Barbara),
we have worked together to form a process that encompasses
creative brainstorming processes within a psychological framework
to help you reflect deep into yourself. This dynamic combination
enables you to re-create your life, your way.

In this unusual book, we present a methodology that is practical
yet creative – through our ReDefinition Model™ you will be given
tools that guide you in a systematic process to redefine yourself –
this redefinition will help you take control of your life as you see fit
– based on a clear vision of your own values and beliefs – free from
the "static" and interference that often occurs when others impose
their values, beliefs and expectations upon our lives. It's now time
to step up and do it your way.

Since change is a constant in life, this process will be the compass
you can use through any life transition.

If you work hard, you will realize the reward and exhilaration of
a life lived intentionally. We wish you an exciting journey!

Barbara McFarland, EdD

Alta Bradford

Chapter 1
The Times They Are A-Changin'

PHOTO: JUPITER IMAGES/BRAND X PICTURES/THINKSTOCK

"If nothing ever changed,
there'd be no butterflies."
– Author Unknown

Racing through our days – Blackberry™ watching, texting, tweeting, or taking care of the people in our lives, we rarely take a moment to catch a breath. Just getting through our routines each day can create an aura of familiarity that lures us into feeling safe and secure. And so it goes until something jolts our equilibrium – a change occurs and it gets us to stop and take notice. It could be that we've hit bottom with our careers, or perhaps a relationship has gone sour. It might even be a health scare. Change of any kind is unsettling. But even though change can be uncomfortable, without it we would become complacent and stagnant.

When dealing with change, perspective is everything. What's *your* attitude toward change? Most of us dread it. We resist it because we feel threatened by it. We want to hang on to the familiar, to cling to what we know. So, we often go through change either as observers or as victims – just floating by. Taking the path of least resistance may be easier but it does take the joy and vibrancy out of our lives.

After the initial feelings of uncertainty pass, those of us who embrace change feel energized. We realize making a change takes a leap of faith. We have to move into the unknown on the hope that something will be better on the other side and that means taking risks. Risks can be minimized by a careful process of redefining who we are in terms of our needs, values, beliefs and personal strengths. It sounds pretty intense. You may ask – "All this just to deal with change?"

Well, let's define our terms. For us, change is a one-time occurrence and can refer to just about anything that happens to us – for example, a change in living arrangements, a change of address, or a change of jobs. Change is a variation or shift from one person, place or thing to another. We, however, are referring to deeper changes that we call transitions. Some transitions are unexpected and strike without warning such as a disabling accident, death of a loved one, divorce, the loss of a job, or an illness. Not all transitions are negative – marriage, birth of a child, a new job can lead us to a redefinition process. Other times, life transitions occur because we find ourselves in a rut. We feel strongly discontented but can't quite put a finger on what we need to do to feel better. These events and situations mean we have to let go of what once was and adapt to a new way of living, no matter how unprepared we feel.

Unlike "change" – which implies that there's a problem to be solved – a need to figure out how best to cope and what we need to do to get through the situation – transitions are multi-layered. They open up a new pathway, giving us an opportunity not only to plan for the actual change, such as a new job or career, reentering the single life again, or dealing with the loss of a loved one, but also to catch our second wind, to begin to discover who we have become and what we really want out of life. It's a time to redefine ourselves.

As reported in a CNN.com online article, one 42-year-old man, who dropped out of college to take a job as a salesperson for an auto supplier, was recently laid off by GM. Having redefined himself, he is now working as an unpaid intern (and happens to be the oldest intern) in the Lansing, Michigan, Mayor's office. He's back to college working to complete his bachelor's degree – and continuing to support a family at the same time. He's happy. His former career paid the bills and afforded him a reasonable lifestyle. His current choices are enriching his life.

So what's happening in your life right now? What transition are you dealing with? Whatever it is, you're making a good decision to read this book — it will give you the tools to live your life intentionally and vibrantly — your way.

The Blank Screen Syndrome

Successfully dealing with transitions entails two steps: First, we have to let go. Secondly, we have to be creative. Letting go of "what once was" is a real challenge even if we weren't very happy with the situation or relationship. We like being comfortable. We become attached to the familiar. The old proverb, "Better the devil you know than the devil you don't know," says it best of all. The other challenge that can paralyze us during a time of transition has to do with the "Blank Screen Syndrome." When we think about what lies ahead, whether it be changing careers or being single, we can't seem to envision exactly what's ahead of us — the unknown. This causes undue anxiety. Consequently, we cling even more tightly to what we had in the past.

Letting go takes time but we can move the process along with a simple strategy — B-R-E-A-T-H-E — just take a deep breath. The first thing taught in self-defense classes is to breathe. When faced with a crisis, we tend to constrict and hold our breath. This is paralyzing — we do the same thing when faced with a transition — we hold on, we tense up. Whenever we feel anxious or frightened about the transition, we need to take several deep breaths. This is the most effective way to disconnect from negative, self-defeating thoughts. By relaxing our minds and bodies, we can think more clearly and that leads us to the second step: It allows us to be creative.

It is our creativity that is the antidote to the Blank Screen Syndrome. For most of us, when we think about what we want our life to be in relation to a transition, we see a "blank screen." For example, let's say you're burned out in your career. As you think about what is next, you're faced with more questions than answers. "What am I better suited for?" "What really interests me?" "How do I justify starting over?" "What if I don't like that?" This can be overwhelming and can halt our progress before we even begin. It's a sure-fire way to be drawn back to the familiar and meander around in the same old ruts.

You may be thinking – "Breathing is easy, but being creative?" Is there a little voice that says, "Not me! I'm not not creative!"? Contrary to popular belief, creativity can be taught. Sure, some people are naturally more "right-brained" thinkers, but there are ways to encourage creativity. Most of us were discouraged from thinking creatively as we attended school, where conformity, discipline, and memorizing facts and figures were promoted. We just need some practice to get used to what it feels like to let ourselves get off the beaten path and explore possibilities.

And practice is what you'll get with this book. By intentionally and consciously breathing and by being creative, you will be able to deal with any life transition. Even though it sounds simple, it's not. It requires hard work and commitment. Framed in positive psychology principles, the redefinition process will tap into your creativity and take you through a dynamic process, giving shape and color to your blank screen, no matter what transition you are facing.

It may seem that psychology and creativity are strange bedfellows. Not the way they are used in this model! Psychology establishes the landmarks of who we've become up to this point in our lives

– these landmarks include our needs, our values, our beliefs and personal traits. Creativity is the energizing spark that gives us momentum and helps us make new connections with what we already know about ourselves. These new connections enable us to see new possibilities. It's recycling what we know about ourselves and redefining and reshaping ourselves into something different. Think about the transformation that takes place in making origami – we begin with a flat piece of paper, and without altering the original shape, we fold and refold to create an entirely new and interesting form.

There's so much about ourselves yet to discover!

How to Use this Book to Reach Redefinition

Your Life. Your Way. ReDefined.™ is written and designed to help you increase your self-awareness by blending creativity and positive psychology principles.

To get you warmed up to the idea that you are a creative being, Chapter 2 will integrate these principles, showing you how both are essential in redefining yourself. You will be given some unique exercises to help you tap into your creative side. These will set the stage for the "Creative Break™" segments that are at the end of most chapters. Although these segments are optional, they are important. They are designed to stimulate new connections that can help you understand and engage more meaningfully with your redefinition. The Creative Breaks™ provide inspiration and motivation throughout the process. Some of these may be more appealing to you than others, so choose what fits best. Chapter 3 presents key focus points to help you stay on track and sustain momentum as you work toward redefinition.

Our ReDefinition Model™, presented in Chapter 4, brings together all the components that are necessary to achieve redefinition. Our model is a "big picture" view of the redefinition process. Think of the model as the picture of the completed puzzle that is on the box. The subsequent chapters give you all the pieces to create your own model.

At the end of Chapters 5 through 9, you will be asked various questions and given exercises to help you make new connections regarding your needs, values, beliefs, personality traits and joys – we will highlight this as the R&R section – Reflect & ReDefine™! The R&R segments are what you will be using to build your redefined self. Consequently, they will need to be done as presented – there is no redefinition without your responses to these sections. Remember, this is not just a "sit back and read" book. Redefinition is about action! The R&R sections are the action steps to the finished product – your redefined self.

You will need a way to record your responses to both the R&R and the Creative Break™ pages. Choose something unique – something out of the ordinary for you. Perhaps a jazzy journal, a zebra-print folder, maybe you want a clipboard or even a box – get something really different from what you normally would use.

At the end of this book by using and synthesizing your responses to the R&R questions, you will have redefined yourself and created a personalized redefinition plan.

We also encourage you to visit our website for additional information and tools related to the redefinition process: www.redefinemyself.com

Let's Get Started!

Chapter 2
Tapping Into Your Creative Juices

PHOTO: HEMERA TECHNOLOGIES/AbleStock/THINKSTOCK

"I'm always thinking about creating. My future starts when I wake up each morning."
– Miles Davis

Psychology and Creativity: Strange Bedfellows

So why apply a creative process to psychology? The answer is "change." Creativity is ALL about change. As we embark upon redefining ourselves, being comfortable with change will make our journey much smoother and more interesting. Creative techniques give us new perspectives and help us sift through and reach the essence of who we are and what we want. At that point, we can begin to experiment and "try on" different aspects of ourselves and see what is most comfortable as we finally find our redefined selves.

Solution focused therapy (SFT) is a psychologically based approach that builds solutions in order to create change. As opposed to traditional therapy which looks at what's wrong with us, SFT is interested in capturing the strengths we have and using them to seek solutions. So, SFT is focused on altering the way a problem is described. The creative process gives us varied and unique ways to change how we view situations. A blend of the two can lead to a reshaping of how we think about ourselves, our future and help to create movement toward desired goals...making a real change in our lives.

Life has always been about change, but these days, the speed of change seems to increase exponentially each year. Though we might often wish that things would return to "the good old days," the reality is that life will keep moving. The more we embrace change, the fuller and more successful we will become. And while change may not always seem welcome, it can be rejuvenating if we meet it head on. The process this book describes gives the framework for doing just that.

Creativity 101

How is creativity defined? Many have tried. Capturing the essence and energy of creativity in mere words is a little bit like trying to "nail JELL-O™ to a wall." As you work through redefining yourself, consider this definition:

"Creativity is the process of looking at things that you already know or already exist about you and opening yourself up to making and seeing new connections with that information."

PHOTO: BRAND X PICTURES/THINKSTOCK

By making new connections, we give ourselves the chance to see new possibilities. We tend to develop mindsets about who we think we are and what we think our capabilities are. Much of what we believe about ourselves is outdated – it comes from parents, teachers, and relatives at a time in our lives when we were quite young. This feedback tends to stick. Thus, our "sense of self" is something we carry with us as our "truth." Think about the "what-you-are-not" messages you received. "You're not athletic." "You'll never get into that college." "You're not that smart." Redefining ourselves is about "stretching" what we believe about ourselves. This expands our possibilities and what we hope to achieve in the future. The way to stretch as far as we can is through creative exercises.

Creativity can take on different meanings based upon our individual experiences and perspectives. This is exactly the right time to embrace our own view of ourselves and with it those possibilities. After all, we are the only ones capable of making those connections. We each have a unique combination. We need to use it to our advantage.

Creativity not only changes what we do but how we do it. Scans show that the brain undergoes changes when engaged in creative exercises. The brain activity evident on the scans is tangible proof of new connections being made. We won't need a brain scan to know that creativity is making a difference because we will experience new insights and even breakthroughs by following creative techniques throughout our redefinition process.

"...but I'm not creative!"

Many of us have probably heard about right- and left-brained thinking. Just because we may tend to be more left-brained doesn't mean that we can't be creative. So let's change that mind-set about ourselves.

Let's define our terms – a left-brained thinker tends to focus more on language, logic, numbers, judgment and "point A to point B" kinds of thoughts. Left-brained thinking probably looks something like this:

Left-brained thinking

Predominately right-brained thinkers typically "zig" when others "zag" because they focus on pictures, patterns, emotions, rhythm and "seeing what happens" – more non-judgmental approaches.

Creative thinking looks more like this:

Right-brained thinking

Both ways of thinking can end up at the same conclusion and very often do. The difference is in the views along the way and the valuable insights that "detours" can reveal.

Creativity happens in lots of places besides in the lives of painters, musicians and photographers. Creativity is an energizing spark that we can apply to many different situations to bring out new perspectives. While there are some people that are more creative than others, it is possible to use techniques to grow our own creative potential. Regardless of the use or the specific approach, most researchers now agree that creativity can be taught and learned.

Creative thinkers tend to be alike in several ways. We need to keep these traits in mind as we engage in creative exercises and look at them as "creative rules" to use when engaging in the Creative Breaks™ at the end of each chapter. They include:

1) Being willing to be wrong and continue to take risks

2) Expressing thoughts and feelings

3) Having a sense of humor about life

4) Trusting and accepting our intuition

Interestingly enough, from a psychological perspective, these same traits are essential to a successful counseling experience. Most people seek counseling because they don't feel good – certain aspects of life have become burdensome – whether it be the stresses of work, love, or health, counseling becomes a way to seek support, increase self-awareness and get on with life. The characteristics above are what contribute to a successful outcome.

With a conscious effort, we can learn to integrate these traits into our approach to redefinition. Most of us, at least those who went to school in the U.S., were taught more "safe" ways of thinking that depended upon conformity and discipline. Throughout this redefinition process, this book presents various creative exercises which will allow us to stretch our established mindsets – even change them completely. This is our chance to "color outside the lines." After all, isn't it time we get to decide what colors we use and whether we want lines at all?

14

"What if..."

Sometimes when confronted with questions that have big consequences, like "What do I want to do with the rest of my life?," it's easy to get stuck or hesitate – to doubt ourselves. The Creative Break™ sections offer exercises and techniques to keep our feet moving! Someone once pointed out that Babe Ruth was the strikeout leader and home-run leader in the same year. The lesson is that in order to hit the home runs, we have to keep swinging. Creativity provides a lot of different ways to keep swinging.

Storming the Brain – A Tool in Redefinition

Earlier we talked about the mindsets we have. One way to crack them open is through brainstorming. Brainstorming is an important creative tool that shows how to "zig rather than zag." People have probably been brainstorming since they first started solving the challenges of life, like inventing fire or making tools. However, the term "brainstorming" is attributed to Alex Osborn. In 1941, Osborn, an advertising executive, defined it as a way to "think up" ideas, primarily in a group setting, to stimulate a freer flow of ideas. He also created a few rules that remain fairly intact today as accepted wisdom. We've applied them to the redefinition process:

- Resist criticizing or judging yourself.
  (Break free from the mindsets.)

- Develop as many ideas as you can.
  (Reshape those mindsets.)

- Be open to feedback from others.
  (Say "Yes, and..." instead of "Yes, but...".)

- Let yourself think as broadly as possible.
  (See beyond those mindsets.)

Brainstorming is what gets us to expand our self-image and our future possibilities. There will be opportunities to brainstorm throughout the redefinition process. Specific strategies will be presented in this chapter and in the Creative Break™ sections. Although the Creative Breaks™ are optional, we strongly encourage you to consider each one carefully and choose which fits you the best – they will help add energy and new insights to your redefinition journey.

Creativity is a great tool for our redefiniton process. As you complete the R&R and Creative Break™ sections throughout the book remember these key points:

CREATIVE TRAITS	BRAINSTORMING RULES
Take risks	Resist criticizing/judging yourself
Express thoughts and feelings	Develop as many ideas as you can
Have a sense of humor	Be open to feedback
Trust and accept your intuition	Think as broadly as possible

Enjoy the journey!

"I was always looking outside myself for strength and confidence, but it comes from within." – **Anna Freud**

PRACTICE makes...

PHOTO: JUPITER IMAGES/COMSTOCK/THINKSTOCK

...a new activity like creativity feel more comfortable and more natural. Forget perfect. Think about it. Haven't you ever heard of a "happy accident"? Artists learn to embrace them. You can too.

Seriously though, your ability to be creative improves as you try new things. Most of us were more creative as children. That was before we were subjected to different ways of learning and began "believing" that we were not creative. You can relearn creativity by practicing. Creativity helps you bend and stretch with change – not break.

Practicing creativity is easy for most of us. Just do the opposite of what you usually do. If you are a left-brain thinker, take an art class, go to a museum, start doing puzzles, or take a different route home. Try making shadow puppets. If you already enjoy creative activities, challenge your brain further. Break out of a rut. Make it your new groove.

Start a list of things you can do to increase your creativity. If you ever find time to be bored, you will be prepared with some ideas.

continued on next page...

continued from previous page...

Here are a few ideas for creative exploration to get you started:

- Watch a different type of movie. How about a foreign film or a documentary? How long has it been since you watched an animated film?
- Read a different type of book. How about going back and re-reading your favorite childhood book? Do you get a new message by reading a familiar book again?
- Switch up your tunes. Listen to a different radio station. Check out some different artists on the Internet.

See where this is going? It's easy.

- Try different clothes.
- Step back and look at your closet. Do you have clothes that are the same color? Try a different colored shirt or blouse.
- Comb your hair differently.
- Have tea instead of coffee.
- Turn off the TV and take a walk.

Along the way if that little voice in your head starts complaining, tell it to take a hike or go fly a kite! Small changes can result in big benefits. As you practice being more creative, you are preparing your mind for big ideas to happen – creativity does favor a prepared mind. Be ready for it!

Try starting a list of activities to try again or for the first time.

I'm going to:

CREATIVE BREAK

"Don't Give Me..."

As you go through your life transition, use brainstorming to get to the heart of what you really want. Write a phrase that focuses on what you want and then fill in the blank with how achieving that goal might make you feel, such as...

"Don't give me a new job, give me control over my day."

"Don't give me a new job, give me satisfaction that I am helping the world."

"Don't give me a new job, give me _____."

The phrase can focus on anything that you want...

"Don't give me a new life, give me _____."

"Don't give me a better relationship, give me_____."

"Don't give me more money, give me _____."

Keep writing your phrase and filling in the blank differently each time. To go faster, make a quick file on the computer of an entire page of the phrase with the blanks. Keep going until you fill a page or two, then stop and evaluate. Fill in the blank with the first thing that comes to mind. Is there a theme to what you are really wanting?

PHOTO: RYAN McVAY/PHOTODISC/THINKSTOCK

Chapter 3
The Pleasure Principle Challenge

"Man's mind, once stretched by a new idea, never regains its original dimensions."

– Oliver Wendell Holmes

We can get stuck very easily as we try to fill in our blank screen. Freud's pleasure principle, which says that we avoid pain and seek pleasure, is the culprit! Redefinition is a challenging process – it can be uncomfortable. Remember: Whenever we deal with any transition, there is discomfort. As long as we keep that in mind, we can prepare for it.

As a way to prepare, we've developed three focus points that will guide you and keep you on track. Just like the directory at the Mall that tells you, "You are here!," these focus points will ground you. They serve as a compass that will keep you from veering off into negative or nonproductive thoughts and actions. These cycles of negativity and dissatisfaction generate the most discomfort when dealing with redefinition.

"The world is but a canvas to the imagination."
– Henry David Thoreau

The Focus Points

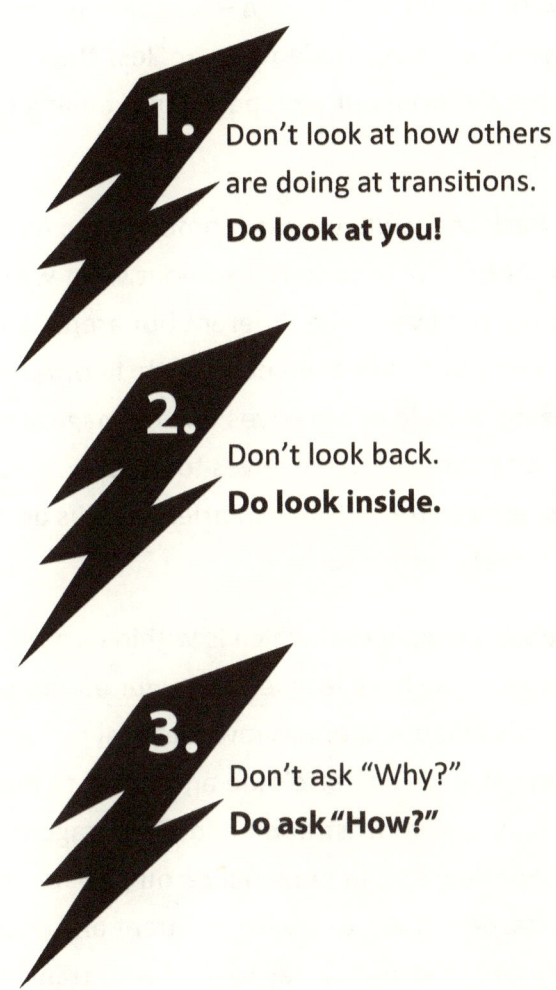

1. Don't look at how others are doing at transitions.
Do look at you!

2. Don't look back.
Do look inside.

3. Don't ask "Why?"
Do ask "How?"

1. Don't look at how others are doing. Do look at you!

Some of us look at others or read about others (generally those others who have what we don't have) in order to measure how we are doing or what we should be doing – financially, physically and relationally. This is not a good idea – comparing ourselves to others often leaves us feeling inadequate or "less than." It also keeps us disconnected from our own path thus keeping us stuck in a cycle of unhappiness.

Others of us sit back and wait...wait for something to happen... something "out there." We tend to think about what we'd like to be or how we'd like our lives to be different but aren't willing to in- vest time and energy to do what we need to do in order to realize our dreams. Gazing outside of ourselves for the magical solution is just as ineffective as comparing ourselves to others. The success of others or hoping for a better future can briefly fire us up and get us moving but is rarely sustainable.

What is sustainable is simply that which is within us already. We need to take what we have learned from our earlier experi- ences and decisions and use them as raw material for redefining ourselves. Looking at someone else's life and trying to make it work for us can only lead to frustration and discouragement. Our own individual experiences and personal resources are unique to us and we must harness them to create a vibrant and intentional future. This is the only successful way to deal with transitions. It is how we begin to give shape and color to that blank screen.

2. Don't look back. Do look inside.

What most of us typically do during a life transition is to look back.

And although this is a good first step, it can be a dangerous one depending on the perspective we take. In reflecting on the past, we tend to focus on what we didn't do, should've done or could've done and this is quickly followed by harsh judgment or criticism of our perceived shortcomings and failures.

Redefinition is not a "do-over" or makeover of you. This suggests that who you are today or what you have experienced is somehow flawed or inadequate. Redefinition is about harnessing your accumulated wisdom and personal resources and synthesizing them to shape you and your future into whatever it is you want them to be.

Our main premise is that we are each a success as we are right now. If we don't believe that about ourselves – no ifs, and or buts about it – our redefinition process will be bogged down with negative energy. Given the cultural and parental influences, most of us aren't satisfied with who we are or who we have become. One antidote to this common problem is to adjust our perspective. Rather than looking at how we can "fix" ourselves to be better or more successful, we need to relish the strengths and qualities that have been the central drivers in out lives – those characteristics that have gotten us through the really tough times. So, whether we are in our 20's or on the back side of our 40's or beyond, we have more successes than we often give ourselves credit for. We spend so much times looking outside ourselves for validation that we forget about our own internal resources. Without faith in ourselves, redefinition is impossible.

3. Don't ask "Why?" Do ask "How?"

Once we embrace who we are and our past experiences, the next challenge we face is the "Why?" question. Since Freud first diplayed his shingle, mental health professionals have been fixated on taking taking their patients down the introspective labyrinth of "Why?," believing that by understanding events or their own motivations, their lives would be more fulfilling and meaningful. Freud's influence had insinuated itself into our collective unconscious so much so that we still cling to the notion that if we can answer the question "Why?," we'll be better off. Consider how this is reinforced in the news every single day. Regardless of the rewards of success, misconduct on the part of celebrities, athletes and politicians is often excused because of the pressures of constantly living in the public arena. And although entertaining the "Why?" of a decision or an event in some situations can be helpful and even interesting, it rarely produces a useful outcome in and of itself. In this case, psychology has kept us chasing our tails.

"Why?" is an obstacle. If we don't like what decisions we made or the outcomes of those decisions, we often get stuck in asking the question "Why?" "Why wasn't I able to figure that out?" "Why didn't I see that coming?" We think that if only we knew the answer to the ubiquitous "Why?," we could avoid future problems or the present discomfort.

The question "Why?" leads us down another slippery slope – it fosters blaming ourselves and/or those around us for what has gone awry in our lives. As we try to figure out the reason for something, it's not uncommon to point to someone as a cause – either other people or even ourselves. "Why did I decide to do that?" "It was my parents' fault," "I should have known better," and so on.

Still, there is something seductive about the question "Why?" It traps us into believing that by analysis and contemplation we can prevent future mistakes and these insights will get us to change and make our lives better. This is magical thinking at its best. Nothing can "get us" to change or make our lives better but our own actions and conscious choices; however, placing the responsibility for the quality of our lives squarely on our own shoulders doesn't jive with our cultural need for quick fixes – our penchant for blaming others for the difficulties we find ourselves in. So, focusing on the "Why?" of our past decisions and their outcomes as well as those events that may have been out of our control keeps us stuck and spinning in a morass of regrets, blame and self-loathing. So where does that leave us?

We have to ask ourselves another question – "How?" The answers generally yield solutions that are focused on our behavior. What gets us moving is the "How?" "How can I make this better or different?" "How can I best cope with this situation?" "How can I learn from this situation?" "How can I utilize my strengths here?" This question forces us to look at the now – the current circumstances we are faced with. Actions do speak louder than words and the key word to get you moving and maintaining momentum is "How."

> "It ain't what they call you, it's what you answer to."
> **– W.C. Fields**

Contrary to what some may believe, creativity and the resulting work of art, be it music, dance, a painting, or a beautifully crafted story, doesn't usually spring fully realized from the artist's imagination. Most artists do have highly developed work habits that they diligently pursue. Years of practice do train your brain and your hand to replicate a beautiful drawing or to play a chord flawlessly. And practice also makes success look "easy."

Most artists, at some point, deal with the actual or metaphoric artistic block of a "blank canvas." Some turn the block into a hurdle that presents a new but conquerable challenge. Others see blocks for what they most often really are – fears. Fear can come through preconceptions, perfectionism, rigidity, or merely focusing on the outcome more intently than the process. At the root of it all there is still fear.

Switch Channels on Your Blank Screen

When fear strikes, here are a few ways to get going again:

• Step back and take a good look.

• Use a different tool. Paint if you usually draw. As you write your redefinition plan, try switching and writing with a colored marker or use your non-dominant hand. Small changes can really make a big impact.

• Try using a different "sense." Image your new life brought to life in music. Put together a mix of "your new soundtrack for life."

• Stop asking for answers. Start listening.

CREATIVE BREAK™

"SECOND CHANCES"

Each day is made up of 86,400 seconds.

Each one of them is another "second chance."

PHOTO: HEMERA TECHNOLOGIES/PHOTOS.COM/THINKSTOCK

29

Chapter 4
The Road Map

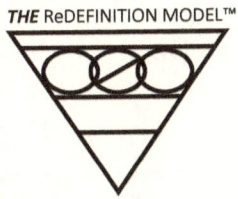

THE ReDEFINITION MODEL™

PHOTO: HEMERA TECHNOLOGIES/PHOTOS.COM/THINKSTOCK

"The only way of discovering the limits of the possible is to venture a little way past them into the impossible."
– Arthur C. Clarke

What's a trip without a map or at least a GPS? As a starting point, we are going to place the ReDefinition Model™ on your blank screen. As you go through the book, you will be giving depth to the model by adding your personal information and insights. We are going to present an overview of the model here and then you will take a deep dive in the chapters that follow.

The ReDefinition MODEL™

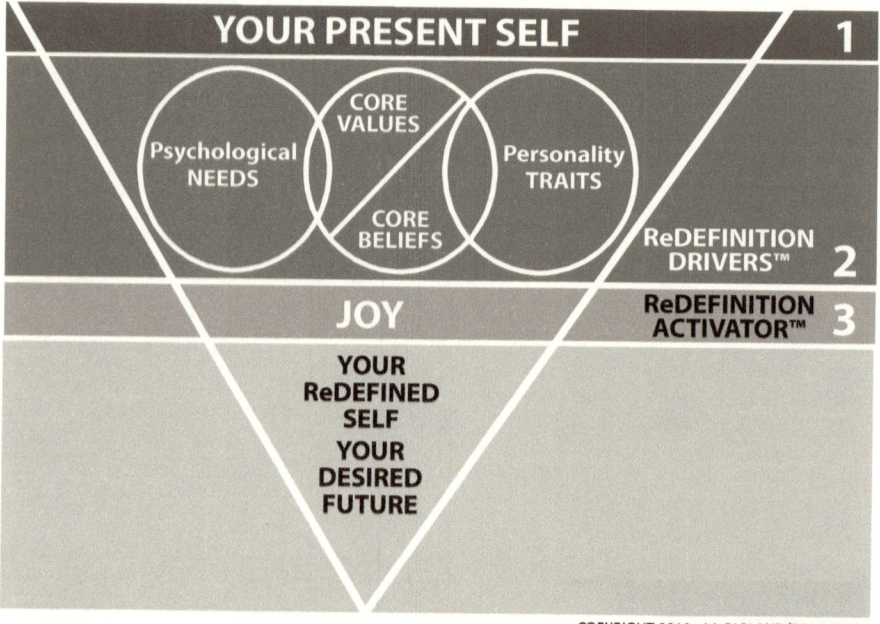

COPYRIGHT 2010 - McFARLAND/BRADFORD

We begin with The Present Self which is you as you are now. The critical assertion here is to accept yourself unconditionally — accept and value all of who you are, warts and all. It's that simple. No judgment, no criticism. No "buts" or "if onlys." Remember, redefinition is not a makeover — it's a reshaping, a reconfiguring of all of who you are at this point in time. The raw material is good, resilient and strong. If you begin the redefinition process with a flawed sense of self, you're bound to end up with the same.

Recognize your worth and celebrate it. The next step is to explore the ReDefinition Drivers™ – that which is uniquely a part of who you are – your needs, your core values/beliefs and your personal traits. We refer to them, in our model, as "drivers" because they serve as dynamic motivators and influencers that can explain your behavior and decisions. By living and working in concert with them, you will not only experience a greater sense of well-being but also will gain a greater sense of control over your future. Let's briefly examine each one separately.

Your needs – of which there are five – love and belonging, power, freedom, fun, and survival – are genetically programmed and motivate you to do what you do. If needs are not met, you will experience discomfort of some type. Remember Freud's pleasure principle. It's a key factor in need satisfaction.

Your core values are deeply held convictions which guide behaviors and decisions and also serve to help you establish your priorities. Core beliefs are not universal truths, but rather your own individual truths. For example, a core belief can be that all people are basically good – a core value would be compassion or altruism. Both values and beliefs tend to reflect how you see life in general. To differentiate them, think of values as more *self-oriented* and beliefs as mostly *externally* directed.

Your personal traits are unique and stable throughout your lifetime. Everyone behaves according to certain distinctive patterns throughout a variety of situations. The Five Factor model of personality (Digman, 1990) gives a framework for identifying your key traits: openness, conscientiousness, agreeableness, extroversion, and emotional stability. Although these traits are fairly stable, it's helpful to reflect on the role they play in your life – being

33

conscious of your traits, values, beliefs and needs will help you chart a more vibrant redefinition.

What gives energy to your drivers is JOY. Your joys make life worth living by increasing your vitality. They also serve to record positive experiences in your memory which can slowly but surely change the interior landscape of your brain structure – so none of us is genetically trapped into unhappiness or misery. Changing this landscape can positively influence how you meet your needs, and make your decisions and choose your priorities (values and beliefs). Needs, values and beliefs and personal traits without joy can lead to repetitive patterns of thought and behavior that keep you stuck and feeling hopeless. So joy is the "ReDefinition Activator™," a force that keeps you "juiced up" for the changes you need to make to realize your redefined self and desired future and to appreciate them when they have been achieved.

These drivers and the activator joy have been a part of your entire life and have shaped who you are and why you are where you are. Chances are for most of your life, they have been unconscious influencers. The demands of family, work and life in general have more than likely distracted you from purposefully living your life in a way that meets your needs, expresses your values/beliefs and allows for joyful experiences. During any major transition, these drivers and the activator joy must become intentional and fully conscious if you are to achieve your goals. What can help you be more conscious and fully present is to B-R-E-A-T-H-E. This strategy not only helps relax you as we talked about in Chapter 1, but it also serves to keep you mindful of the present moment. Our awareness can only focus on one thing at a time – so if we breathe with awareness, we will automatically disconnect from our thoughts which are usually negative and worrisome and deal with the future or the past.

We believe it's essential to have clarity with each of these in order to create a future and a redefined self that will lead to greater fulfillment and personal satisfaction. The challenge is making the time to do the reflective work needed to understand, modify and re-evaluate how each of these are working for you now and how you plan to use them to your advantage in redefining yourself.

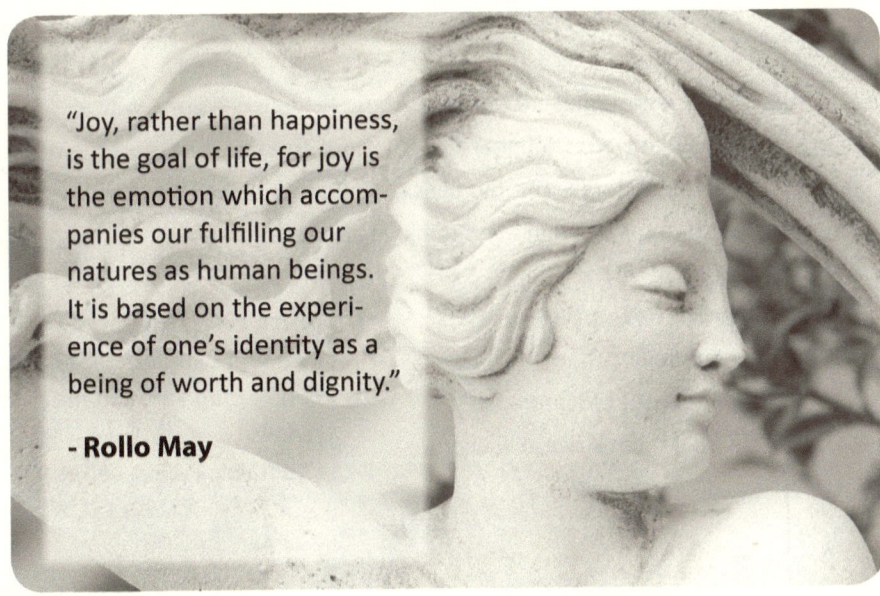

"Joy, rather than happiness, is the goal of life, for joy is the emotion which accompanies our fulfilling our natures as human beings. It is based on the experience of one's identity as a being of worth and dignity."

- **Rollo May**

CREATIVE BREAK™

As you progress through the ReDefinition Model™, we'll ask you to use pictures to represent your thought and feelings. This will help you make decisions and create a mental picture of your desired future.

Pictures are a far superior way to explain your thoughts. Using pictures helps you "project" your thoughts which are primarily image-based. Seeing pictures also helps you remember and internalize your goals. You retain only about 15% of what you hear and can recall about 60% of what you see.

Using a metaphor to represent various ideas is a great way to loosen up your thoughts and get more creative. The most memorable metaphors evoke our senses. You probably say similar phrases all the time without even thinking about it.

Touch or Temperature

- I'm *boiling* mad.
- Find your old *flame*.
- Give them a *warm* welcome.

Touch or Texture

- He was a *smooth* talker.
- She's *rough* around the edges.
- Your voice is like *velvet*.

Sight or Light
- I'm so *blue*.
- He *lights* up my life.
- I *see* what you mean.

Smell
- Love *stinks*!
- Life smells *sweet*.
- They are *stinking* rich.

Taste
- You have great *taste!*
- You're *sweet!*
- Aren't you *spicy!*

Sound / Hearing
- Let's end on a high *note*.
- Your voice is *music* to my ears.
- That's a pretty *loud* shirt!

Now, let's practice using descriptive language, like a metaphor, and pictures to bring your thoughts to life. This exercise will help you begin to think more creatively.

First, choose one of these questions. You can try them all, but focus on one at a time.

– How would you describe a typical day in your current life? Is it a wild ride on a *bucking* bronco or *smooth* sailing on the mirror-like surface of a lake?

– How would achieving redefinition make you feel? Like a flower whose *soft* petals are opening up to the sun or a *roaring* lion claiming his territory?

– As you work toward redefinition, what animal would you choose to describe yourself? Are you *an ant* marching confidently to your goal and carrying 100 times your weight in success or are you *a duckling* turning into *a swan?*

Use both words and pictures to describe your answer. Tear pictures and words from old magazines. Paste them on a poster board or tape them inside your journal.

Chapter 5
You're Right Now!

"Trust yourself.
Create the kind of self
that you would be happy
to live with all your life.
Make the most of your-
self by fanning the tiny,
inner sparks of
possibility into flames
of achievement."
– Golda Meir

As we go through a transition – be it a divorce, job loss, promotion or even relocation, it's not uncommon to feel waves of self-doubt – our confidence and self-esteem wane. The change brings with it unfamiliarity – new terrain to traverse. What if I fail? Do I really have what it takes to succeed?

Trial and error is how most of us have gotten through life's problems. Yet, many of us still are fearful of making a mistake. We doubt our own experience. This is particularly true of perfectionists who believe failure is unacceptable. They would rather hang onto an early success, that which worked in the past, rather than venture out into the unknown. So, rather than take a risk, fear keeps us from testing our inner resolve, from building our self-confidence, of seeing what we really are made of. Therefore, the first step in building confidence and self-esteem is going after what we want, no matter what.

The way to get momentum going is to start with the premise that You're Right Now. We need to dump the droning loops of negative self-talk and the old tapes from when some relative said we were lazy or not so smart. The brain spits out 70,000 thoughts a day! Most of which are repetitive. With practice and determination we can control those thoughts that weaken our confidence. We do have a choice.

Do you have ANTs or PETs?

Yakety, yak, yak, yak... Does that little voice in your head talk nice to you or is it a real NAG? We all have a little voice of our own that sometimes chimes in and cuts off our confidence like a bad haircut. Your subconscious beliefs can be very powerful. Those thoughts are called ANTs or PETs. ANTs are "automatic negative thoughts." PETs are "personal-enhancing thoughts." Just remember that you don't have to believe every thought that you have! Talk back to your crazy distorted thoughts. Thoughts LIE! A LOT. Have some "ANTeaters" handy. That's what to call the tactics that you can keep handy for whenever ANTs show up.

Here are a few "ANTeaters" to change those pesky ANTs to PETs:

- Ask yourself, "Is this thought true?" It's simple, yet effective.
- Change the way that you answer. Instead of "yes, but..." try "yes and...". Give your creativity room to grow.
- For persistent ANTs, turn the thought around. For example, if you are assigned a challenging project and you are telling yourself that you will fail, think of positive outcomes. Like this. "I will learn a new skill by trying this project." "This project gives me a chance to try public speaking." "My boss gave me this project because he/she has confidence in my abilities." Keep listing positive outcomes until you drown the ANT! This can get you past creative blocks and change "Why?" to "Why not?"

Another challenge to confidence and self-esteem is personalization. This is when we take a situation and blame ourselves for its occurrence and, generally, these are not positive situations. For example, let's say someone gets downsized – she can either blame herself for not having what it takes to keep a job ("Wah! Wah! Poor me!") and feel like a failure or she can accept that lots of people lose their jobs and begin seeking other employment options. People with lower self-esteem tend to personalize – their perspective is skewed toward self-blame, having little objectivity about the situation at hand. Needless to say, we're talking about taking appropriate responsibility for situations that happen to us and then moving on. People who personalize tend to view unforeseen and unwanted situations as a personal affront to their very souls. We each have a rich reservoir of personal strengths and traits. We have used them to navigate our lives thus far. It's all about connecting with them. So regardless of what stage of life we're in, if we've made it to adulthood, we've learned a lot about ourselves – either through life experiences, feedback from others, personal growth learning, and so on. In the process of redefining ourselves, we have to honor our present self – who we have become – who we are today, without judgment.

The Present Self is at the very top of the model – it's that important. Do you believe that you are a success as you are right now? If not, adjust your attitude. In the redefinition process this segment of the model is more about attitude than about action steps. However, there are some things you can do to rewire any negative thoughts you have about yourself.

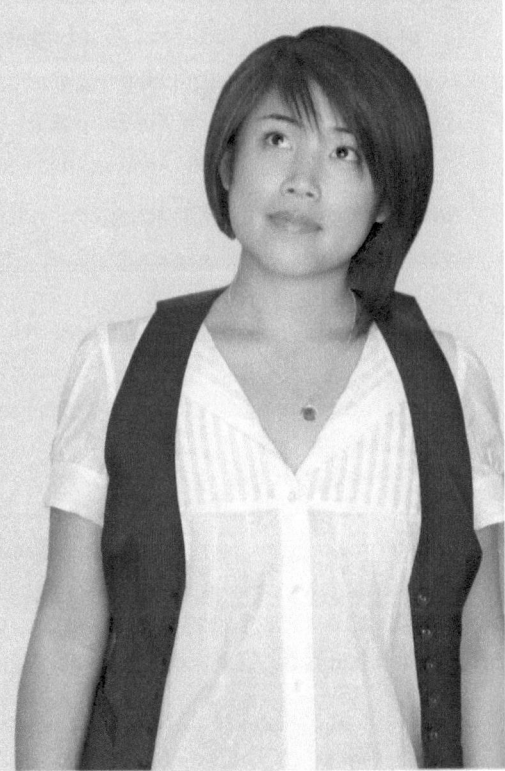

Yakety, yak, yak, yak... Does that little voice in your head talk nice to you or is it a real NAG?

PHOTO: CREATAS IMAGES/THINKSTOCK

Your Life. Your Way. ReDefined.

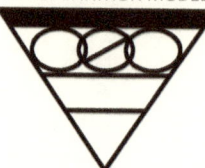

**Reflect&
ReDefine™**

*YOUR PRESENT SELF IN
THE* ReDEFINITION MODEL™

Chapter 5 Exercise
Your Present Self

1. Identify three times in your life when you felt great about yourself.
   a)
   b)
   c)

If you are unable to answer question 1, try this exercise. If you can answer question 1, continue to questions 2 and 3.

For one day, write down all of your self-talk messages – identify the ANTs and change them to PETs. Raise your awareness each day and consciously increase your PETs! Tune into your body to see how different you feel physically when you're thinking positively about yourself. Keep practicing! It will make a difference if you keep at it.

OR, Answer these questions:

Considering your family, teachers, friends, etc., who were the people who believed in you the most?

What do you suppose they saw in you?

How can you live each and every day being what they believed you to be?

---

2. What were you doing when you felt great about yourself? What is about doing this activity that makes you feel good about who you are?

3. How can you recapture those feelings?

   Sit quietly and visualize the happiest you've been with yourself. Do this a few times a week.

PHOTO: HEMERA TECHNOLOGIES/PHOTO OBJECTS.COM/THINKSTOCK

How to Draw a Squirrel

Once there was a young boy who loved to draw. He especially loved the school days when his teacher would allow the students to draw during story time. One day the story was about a squirrel so the little boy drew a squirrel on his paper. He imagined that the squirrel was lively and loved to hide among the leaves in the big oak tree. The little boy thought this picture was the best that he had ever drawn.

That day, when the teacher came to look at his finished drawing, she got very quiet. Finally, she said, "This is wrong. Squirrels cannot be green! Don't you know that?"

The little boy tried to explain but he did not have the right words. From that day forward, he never felt the same joy about drawing. Each time he thought about drawing, he heard the voice of that teacher telling him that his drawing was wrong. He could never bring himself to start another drawing.

No one sees the world quite as you do. What color would your squirrel be? How long has it been since you just sat down and thought about how you look at the world? Have you ever done that? Whose voice do you hear when you want to try something new, different or fun?

continued on next page...

45

continued from previous page...

Whose voice do you hear when you want to try something new, different or fun? Does your voice "block" you from getting started?

What creative activity have you forgotten about doing? Think beyond drawing or painting. How about music? Cooking? Wood-working? Origami? Gardening? Sewing? Knitting? Writing?

You don't have to do something that is labeled as "artistic" to be creative. Opening yourself to learning about the world, exploring other cultures or just watching a genre of movie that you don't normally watch can open your eyes to new possibilities.

Opening yourself to new experiences doesn't have to be hard work. Start simple. Try a new restaurant. To choose, open the yellow pages to restaurants and choose the fifth one down the list or the eighth one. Or type something into your computer's search engine like "tasty new restaurant in (insert the name of your city) gets rave reviews" and see what pops up!

"Creativity comes from trust. Trust your instincts. And never hope more than you work." **– Rita Mae Brown**

Looking Closer
at What Really Matters

98% of life success is just showing up.

Are you showing up for yourself?

Give yourself time each day to focus and
to recharge your creative energy.

Recharge by going to see the arts,
reading, doing puzzles, etc.

Find the activities that appeal to you!

PHOTO: STOCKBYTE/THINKSTOCK

47

Chapter 6
What Makes Us Tick

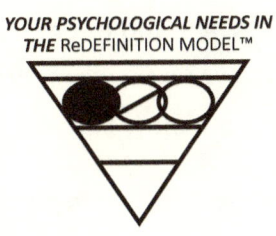

PHOTO: BRAND X PICTURES/THINKSTOCK

"Our necessities never
equal our wants."

– Benjamin Franklin

Consider that every day, each of us is exposed to anywhere from a few hundred to a few thousand marketing messages, depending on who is counting. From television, relentless pop-up Internet ads, cars and buses whizzing by telling us to buy this or that, to logos all over our clothes, we are constantly being told what we should want and need. Is it any wonder that most of us, if asked, would have difficulty telling our needs from our wants? If asked, would you know?

Take a few moments to jot down what is a "need" and what is a "want."

		NEED	WANT
1.	shoes	☐	☐
2.	designer suit	☐	☐
3.	water	☐	☐
4.	large apartment	☐	☐
5.	bed	☐	☐
6.	meaningful relationships	☐	☐
7.	lottery tickets	☐	☐
8.	being loved	☐	☐
9.	golf clubs	☐	☐
10.	a sense of belonging to others	☐	☐
11.	club membership	☐	☐
12.	freedom to think and do as I wish	☐	☐
13.	concert tickets	☐	☐
14.	learning	☐	☐
15.	medicine	☐	☐
16.	achieving something	☐	☐
17.	recognition	☐	☐

(ANSWERS: 3, 6, 8, 10, 12, 14, 16, 17 – are all needs – psychological needs)

These needs are critical to the quality of life we can enjoy. When fulfilled, they give us a greater sense of well-being and personal satisfaction. As for those golf clubs (in the list on the previous page) – we may think they will meet a psychological need and give us a greater sense of well-being, but our core values will determine just how important it is to actually buy them. Having clarity regarding our core values and beliefs can help us sort out how best to meet these needs. Before we do that, let's look at what these five needs are.

We are motivated and driven by five basic needs. These needs are actually built into our genetic make-up. And all of our choices and behaviors are based upon the urgency to satisfy these needs:

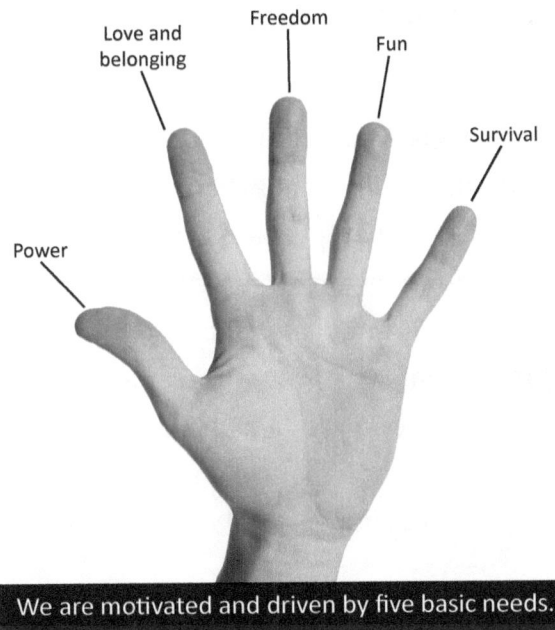

Love and belonging

Freedom

Fun

Survival

Power

We are motivated and driven by five basic needs.

Like fingerprints, the degree to which each of these needs is met is unique to each of us. Let's use the example of two siblings: One has a strong need for power and meets this need by excelling in school and sports; the other sibling has a strong need for belonging and, thus, strives to build and maintain a strong social circle of friends. Two individuals behaving in very different ways as a result of what they each need.

Even though these needs are at the very core of our being, the behaviors and values that we use to meet them can and usually do change depending upon life stage or circumstances. Let's return to our siblings: As the sibling with the need for power matures, doing well academically is replaced with a strong desire to excel in a career. The other sibling continues to be highly social but, with maturity, chooses a career that allows for significant contact with people.

So, as we go through life we are driven to meet these needs and make decisions to that end. The question is whether or not we are consciously making choices to satisfy our needs or doing so by default. Most of us do so by default – without thinking whether or not the action taken is one that will lead to our well-being. We often choose jobs or mates without thinking about how well our needs will be met. Someone with a high need for belonging won't do well with working at a home office day in and day out – just as someone with a high need for survival would be anxious at starting a business.

Consequently, it is essential to review and determine how important each need is to us and how we are meeting these needs and what we might do differently as we redefine ourselves.

Let's explore each of our needs.

For each need, you will rate your need "strength" – that is, how strong of a need this is for you. You will also rate your need "satisfaction" – that is, how much this need is currently being satisfied at this point in time.

The Need for Survival/Safety

Food, clothing and shelter are not dominant forces in our lives. But survival needs can transcend the basics and relate to safety and security issues. Some examples of a survival needs can be:

Which one fits you?	Yes	No
Having medical insurance		
Living and/or working in a safe place		
Having job security		
Being financially sound		

Rate Your Need "STRENGTH" for Survival/Safe-

(-) Low				High (+)
1	2	3	4	5

Rate Your Need *"Satisfaction"* for Survival/Safety

(-) Low				High (+)
1	2	3	4	5

The Need to Belong: Love, Share, Cooperate

Nearly as important to us as the need for survival is the need to belong – the need for friends, family and love. It's that closeness and sense of caring and love that adds important meaning for our lives. A Pulitzer Prize winner once said that his need to be loved was what motivated him to be the best in his field.

Some examples include:

Which one fits you?	Yes	No
Having a strong network of friends		
Belonging to a group or community		
Giving and receiving love		
Being a part of a team at work		
Feeling accepted by others		

Rate Your Need "STRENGTH" to Belong, Love, Share and Cooperate

(-) Low				High (+)
1	2	3	4	5

Rate Your Need *"Satisfaction"* to Belong, Love, Share and Cooperate

(-) Low				High (+)
1	2	3	4	5

The Need for Power

The need for power has to do with increasing personal status and prestige – having the latest car or getting a promotion can be a way to meet this need. Self-esteem is related to the need for power – if we feel inadequate we are more likely to seek ways to feel better about ourselves. Sometimes those ways are productive, like getting an advanced degree, or destructive, like working 80 hours a week to outshine everyone else on the team.

Which one fits you?	Yes	No
Achieving		
Receiving awards/being acknowledged		
Attaining education/training		
Being assigned highly visible projects at work		

The Need for Power (continued)

Rate Your Need "STRENGTH" for Power

(-) Low				High (+)
1	2	3	4	5

Rate Your Need *"Satisfaction"* for Power

(-) Low				High (+)
1	2	3	4	5

The Need for Freedom

We want freedom to choose to live our lives as we see fit. In regard to work, we need autonomy and flexibility. In regard to relationships, we need to reasonably pursue our individual goals and appropriately express our thoughts and feelings.

Which one fits you?	Yes	No
Freedom of speech		
Freedom to choose who I associate with		
Freedom of worship		
Reasonable autonomy at work		

Rate Your Need "STRENGTH" for Freedom

(-) Low				High (+)
1	2	3	4	5

Rate Your Need *"Satisfaction"* for Freedom

(-) Low				High (+)
1	2	3	4	5

The Need for Fun

Fun is a basic genetic function because it's the way we learn and play. The most obvious manifestation of having fun is laughter. Research shows laughter affects our biochemistry by increasing antibodies, decreasing levels of stress hormones and decreasing heart rate. Having fun is a great stress releaser and serves to re-energize us.

Which one fits you?	Yes	No
Learning new things		
Laughing		
Pursuing an interesting new goal		

Rate Your Need "STRENGTH" for Fun

(-) Low				High (+)
1	2	3	4	5

Rate Your Need "Satisfaction" for Fun

(-) Low				High (+)
1	2	3	4	5

So, what insights have you gained about your needs by rating the strength and satisfaction of each one? Do you have gaps, in any specific need, between the strength and satisfaction? If so, what can you do to close the gap? Remember to capture your thoughts.

Redefinition and Needs

When our needs are not being met, we experience frustration, anger, impaired productivity, burn-out, and irritability, to mention a few of the consequences. This can lead to job loss and serious.

relationship and health problems. So, we need to know and understand what our needs are, how they might conflict and how best to constructively meet them.

Needs may conflict with one another, creating stress and anxiety. Take for example, if we have a strong need for power, working overtime to receive a highly visible promotion might limit the time we spend with our loved ones thus interfering with our need for belonging. What do we do? Keep working long hours while mollifying the complaints of our family? Give up the promotion to be more available at home? This decision will be influenced by the intensity of the need as well as by our value system.

In redefining yourself, knowing your needs will help you make decisions that will be satisfying and rewarding.

"Creativity requires the courage to let go of certainties."
– Erich Fromm

Reflect&
ReDefine™

YOUR PSYCHOLOGICAL NEEDS IN
THE ReDEFINITION MODEL™

Chapter 6 Exercise
Summary of Your Psychological Needs

To summarize, on a scale of 1-5,
with 1 being weak and 5 being strong,
rate the intensity of each need:

Survival   (-)   1   2   3   4   5   (+)

(Are you a risk taker? If so, you may have a lower survival need.)

Fun   (-)   1   2   3   4   5   (+)

(Do you enjoy learning? Do you laugh a lot and enjoy humorous movies, books, etc.? If so, you may have a high need for fun.)

Freedom   (-)   1   2   3   4   5   (+)

(Do you dislike following rules and conforming? Do you dislike structure? If so, you have a high need for freedom.)

Love & Belonging   (-)   1   2   3   4   5 (+)

(How much are you willing to give of your time, yourself, your attention? The more you're willing to give the higher the need.)

Power   (-)   1   2   3   4   5   (+)

(Do you often want your own way, have the last word? Are you extremely competitive, need attention and recognition? If so, you may have a high need for power.)

At this time, which are your strongest needs? Are they being met adequately? If not, how can you best meet them? Are any needs in conflict with one another? What can you do to balance them?

_____

_____

_____

_____

_____

_____

_____

_____

In redefining yourself, meeting your needs will be an essential element of creating your redefinition plan.

PHOTOS: JUPITER IMAGES/BRAND X PICTURES/THINKSTOCK

"To live a creative life, we must lose our fear of being wrong." – **Joseph Chilton Pierce**

Bring Your Needs to Life.

PHOTO: COMSTOCK/THINKSTOCK

Energize your redefinition process by creating a more tangible expression of your needs. Choose the media that appeals most to you. Or do them all. Be sure to capture any "Aha!" moments!

PICTURE IT! There are two ways to do this activity. If you have photos that express a particular need, use those to create a collage. Add words to explain your feelings about your needs. Set it up like a story to explain how the need is being met right now in your life. Add notes on the collage to remind you of the feelings and what others saw in you. Keep the collage with your journal to remind yourself as you work on your redefinition.

NAME YOUR TUNE! Create a "soundtrack" for one or more of your needs and choose a song for each. Put it on your phone or iPod. Play it when you need a boost.

BE A STAR! What movie or music video represents your needs? Or, if one of your needs were made into a movie, who would play your part? What about the other parts?

See How the Cookie Crumbles…

Here is a simple exercise to stimulate some spontaneous thoughts and just have some fun.

Get some fortune cookies and randomly choose one to break and read the fortune. Write the fortune down in your notebook. Think about these questions and record your thoughts.

- How does this fortune "speak" to my present life?
- How does it relate to my dreams and plans for the future?
- What ideas come to mind?
- What pictures does the fortune bring to mind?

Here are some other things to try:

Break two more cookies. Add the two new fortunes to the first one. Try to make up a story or possible scenario for your future using the three fortunes.

Write your own fortune. What message would you like to receive for your career, relationships or other goals?

If you don't want to go buy cookies, just "google" any of these phrases – "fortune cookie sayings," "fortune cookie messages" or "fortune cookie ideas." You will find websites that give you lists of sayings. Some offer lists of fortune cookie sayings that are sorted into different topics like love, business or motivational sayings.

If fortune cookies don't interest you, try opening a dictionary to any page and without looking at the page, put your finger on a word and then read it. What is your first thought? How does the word relate to your present life? You can also use a book of quotations or whatever book might inspire you, such as the Bible.

Just let yourself enjoy the unpredictability of not knowing what you will receive.

Chapter 7
What Really Matters

"It is only with the heart
that one can see rightly,
what is essential is
invisible to the eye."
— **Antoine de Saint-Exupéry**

PHOTO: JUPITER IMAGES/PHOTOS.COM/THINKSTOCK

Core values and beliefs are two more groups of drivers that influence us. Think of these as part of an internal GPS system that guides our decisions. Just like brands and companies have core values that they use to shape their culture and define how they interact with customers, we also use them to set priorities and make decisions. If we are living in harmony with our core values and beliefs, we will experience less stress and feel a greater sense of satisfaction in our lives.

Unlike needs which are genetically programmed, values and beliefs are learned. Beliefs are formed earlier in our lives. We believe in God, in Santa Claus, or the Easter Bunny. We believe from such a young age because we copy the beliefs of others. Our values are formed as we mature but are also influenced by our parents, extended family members, teachers, peers and institutions as well.

Core Values
- direct us and keep us on the path that's right for us
- determine what's important to us during decision-making
- provide a sense of meaning to what we do

We can look at valuing as an action – as an expression. Values are revealed in our attitudes about the worth of people, concepts, or things. For example, we might value travelling, a fast car, ocean living, friendship, personal comfort, or family. Values are important as they influence our behavior to weigh the importance of alternatives. For example, we might value autonomy more than we do teamwork, thus when faced with the choice of working independently or on a work team, we would favor the former.

Beliefs are our truths, our personal rules for living, and our view of the way life is. Beliefs are what our values are based on. We hold certain beliefs about the world and our values spring from those beliefs. If we believe all people are created equal, our values might be justice, diversity, and/or democracy. Values are closer to us – we live them daily with our words, our thoughts, our behaviors and our decisions. Using the example above, believing all people are created equal, valuing diversity, we might choose to send our children to an ethnically diverse school or live in a diverse community.

Core Beliefs

- direct us and keep us
- serve as guidelines for the *raison d'être* of our lives
- give meaning to our lives
- influence our expectations

Our beliefs, however, although important, are not as entwined in our daily lives. Beliefs have to do with our future – with our expectations. Our ability to get what we want in life is strongest when what we want is what we expect. Our expectations spring from our core beliefs. If we believe life should be fair, we might expect justice in all situations. Bringing it closer to home, if we believe we deserve a promotion, we expect to get it. Our sense of fairness comes into play. If someone else gets the job, we will experience anger – when our expectations are not met, we become angry. Many people are angry most of the time because their expectations about life, love, work, etc. (which spring from their beliefs), are not being met. That's why knowing our beliefs is so critical in the redefinition process.

On the other hand, values deal with our present. And because values can change much more quickly than beliefs, they are far more personal. Let's say we believe in a Higher Power but don't see a value in praying or in attending services. Then we are unexpectedly diagnosed with a serious medical condition or someone we love is. That situation could change our value related to prayer, to recognizing the existence of a Higher Power, and so on. This would result in actively praying, going to a service, etc. Values can change.

With unmet expectations, anger arises and when we are not living within our value system, we experience stress – frustration, anxiety, even depression. Thus, doing an inventory of our values in the redefinition process not only gives us a sound basis for the decisions we might need to make but also allows for a greater sense of well-being.

In redefining ourselves, we need to decide which of the earlier learned values and beliefs are ones that are consistent with who we have become. If we don't, we may find ourselves living our lives according to the values and beliefs of other people or institutions instead of being true to our own selves.

Reflect&
ReDefine™

YOUR CORE BELIEFS & CORE VALUES IN
THE ReDEFINITION MODEL™

Chapter 7 Exercise
Taking a Closer Look at Personal
Core Values & Beliefs

Choose 20 values, then 10 and then finally 5 and then rank them in order of importance to you.

Accessibility	Discovery	Inner peace	Responsibility
Accomplishment	Diversity	Innovation	Safety
Accountability	Duty	Integrity	Security
Accuracy	Education	Joy	Self-reliance
Achievement	Efficiency	Justice	Sincerity
Attitude	Empowerment	Knowledge	Stability
Authority	Equality	Leadership	Strength
Autonomy	Excellence	Learning	Style
Beauty	Fairness	Loyalty	Success
Challenge	Faith	Money	Tolerance
Change	Family	Optimism	Tranquility
Purity	Freedom	Peace	Trust
Commitment	Fun	Popularity	Truth
Communication	Generosity	Power	
Community	Giving/charity	Prosperity/wealth	
Courage	Gratitude	Punctuality	
Cooperation	Hard work	Recognition	
Creativity	Honesty	Reliability	
Determination	Hope	Respect	
Discipline	Humor		

My top 5 core values, ranked from most important to least important.

(+)   1.

        2.

        3.

        4.

(-)   5.

Identify your core beliefs in each of these areas.

We've given some examples.

CATEGORY	CORE BELIEF	How this impacts my decisions
1. Myself	1. I am not that smart.	1. I tend to be more cautious in my decisions.
2. Other People	2. People are basically good.	2. I tend to be trusting of people I first meet.
3. Work	3. I have a strong work ethic.	3. I tend to work first and play later.

CATEGORY	CORE BELIEF	How this impacts my decisions
1. Myself		
2. Other People		
3. Work		
4. Add others (for example, family, spirituality, etc.)		

Sorting Out Your Core Beliefs and Values

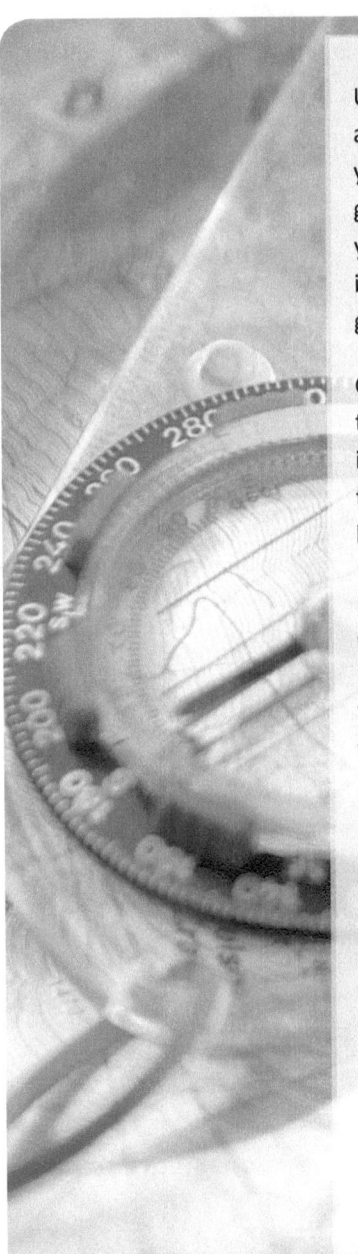

Use your core beliefs and values as filters to decide what fits in your life. Look at your overall goal. Do all your ideas support your goal? Either throw out the ideas that don't fit or revise your goal and exclude other ideas.

Or, do you have several ideas that are pieces of one bigger idea? If so, group them or put them in order under that one bigger idea.

Find three pictures to illustrate each of your final five core beliefs and values. Tear them from old magazines. Think about these questions.

- Do you have too many ideas?

- Which one shows up the most in your life?

- Is there one core belief or value that you want to strengthen? Brainstorm ways to increase how you live that belief or value now. Would you live that core belief or value differently in your redefined life? How?

PHOTO: ABLESTOCK/ABLESTOCK.COM/THINKSTOCK

69

Take a Line for a Walk

As you spend time thinking about the questions that help you form your newly redefined self, it is helpful to take mental breaks. When was the last time, you just let your mind wander and put pencil to paper to doodle. Did you know that doodling actually can increase your mind's ability to notice and remember rather ordinary, boring information by almost 30%? A researcher at the University of Plymouth, UK, discovered this phenomenon in a recent study. The very basic explanation of this theory is that doodling prevents daydreaming from igniting cortical processes in the brain that would otherwise interfere with paying attention. Give it a try!

"Finish" the random lines on this page by continuing to doodle. Turn them into wherever your doodling takes you.

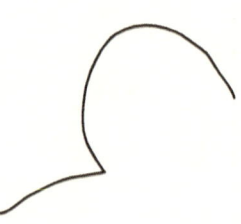

Find Your Muse

A muse can inspire you to see new ways to think about your life. Who inspires you? It can be someone you know or a famous person. If your muse is someone famous, read about them and become familiar with their work. You will probably be surprised to find out that they also struggle with creative expression. Some of the most successful artists have to overcome the highest hurdles.

Try any of these ways to find a muse:

– **Google it!** If you are a woman who wants to start a business from your home try googling a phrase like "woman who started a successful business from home."

– **Read about it!** Look for autobiographies. The subjects don't have to be famous to be inspiring.

– **Listen for it!** Check out Public Radio online at npr.org for podcasts of shows that talk about peoples' lives and how they dealt with personal challenges. Two shows in particular come to mind – "This I Believe" and "Fresh Air" with Terry Gross.

Chapter 8
What We Show The World

PHOTO: COMSTOCK/THINKSTOCK

"To think creatively, we must be able to look afresh at what we normally take for granted."

– George Kneller

As we work toward redefinition, we must have an awareness and appreciation of our personality traits to achieve our goals. This next focus area in the model is a vital part of our redefinition. Though some psychologists say that our personality is pretty well formed by the age of 5, we still need to examine and acknowledge its influence and how we present ourselves to the world.

We need to think of our personality as a basic foundation from which we behave. This is how others might describe their experience of us. People around us may not be able to describe our core beliefs or values but they likely can describe our personality. We have probably described others in terms of their personality, as well, by saying that someone is "outgoing" or has a "strong" personality.

In order to describe personality in a consistent way, Digman (1990) developed the Five Factor model of personality.

The five key traits in his framework are:

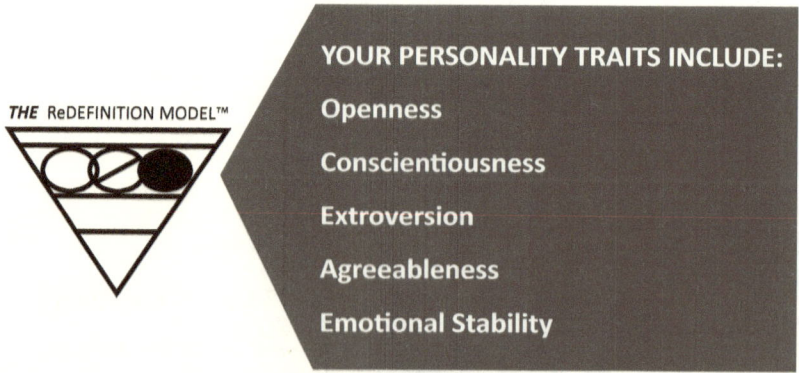

THE ReDEFINITION MODEL™

YOUR PERSONALITY TRAITS INCLUDE:

Openness

Conscientiousness

Extroversion

Agreeableness

Emotional Stability

To help you look at your traits, we've modified the model and are asking you to rate yourself on each trait. It would be interesting to ask significant others to rate you as well so you could compare the results.

74

As you go through each personal trait, read each description and rate yourself, trying to capture your first thought. Avoid editing yourself and just go on to the next trait until you have completed rating yourself on all five traits.

Openness – In pursuit of the next, new thing!

Openness is a general appreciation for art, emotion, adventure, unusual ideas, imagination, curiosity, and variety of experience. The trait distinguishes imaginative people from down-to-earth, conventional people.

Rate yourself:

Openness/Intellect (inventive / curious vs. cautious / conservative). Appreciation for art, emotion, adventure, unusual ideas, curiosity, and variety of experience.

(-) Low		Rate yourself		High (+)
1	2	3	4	5

People who rate themselves high on this trait usually say:

☐   I can describe anything for you...in many different ways.

☐   I have a vivid imagination.

☐   I spend time reflecting on things.

☐   I like to think about how things fit together and imagine new things.

☐   I have a good imagination.

Conscientiousness – This is definitely "in the box!"

Conscientiousness is a tendency to show self-discipline, act dutifully, and aim for achievement. The trait shows a preference for planned rather than spontaneous behavior. It influences the way in which we control, regulate, and direct our impulses.

Rate yourself:

Conscientiousness (efficient / organized vs. easy-going /careless). A tendency to show self-discipline, act dutifully and aim for achievement; planned rather than spontaneous behavior.

(-) Low		Rate yourself		High (+)
1	2	3	4	5

People who rate themselves high on Conscientiousness usually say:

☐   I'm always prepared.

☐   I like to follow a schedule.

☐   My motto is, "Work before play."

☐   I like order.

☐   I like everything in its place.

Extroversion – It's about being with people!

Extroversion is characterized by positive emotions, urgency, and the tendency to seek out stimulation and the company of others. The trait is marked by pronounced engagement with the external world.

Extroverts enjoy being with people, and are often perceived as full of energy. They tend to be enthusiastic, action-oriented individuals who are likely to say "Yes!" or "Let's go!" to opportunities for excitement. In groups they like to talk, assert themselves, and draw attention to themselves.

Introverts lack the social exuberance and activity levels of extroverts. They tend to seem quiet, low-key, deliberate, and less involved in the social world. Their lack of social involvement should not be interpreted as shyness or depression. Introverts simply need less stimulation than extroverts and more time alone. They may be very active and energetic, simply not socially.

Rate yourself:

Extroversion (outgoing / energetic vs. shy / withdrawn). Energy, positive emotions, urgency, and the tendency to seek stimulation in the company of others.

(–) Low		Rate yourself		High (+)
1	2	3	4	5

People who rate themselves high on Extroversion usually say:

☐ I am the life of the party. The party doesn't really start until I arrive.

☐ I don't mind being the center of attention.

☐ I feel more comfortable being with people.

☐ I am usually the first to start a conversation.

☐ I am always talking...probably in my sleep, too!

Agreeableness – "Can't we all just get along?"

Agreeableness is a tendency to be compassionate and cooperative rather than suspicious and antagonistic toward others. The trait reflects individual differences in general concern for social harmony. Agreeable individuals value getting along with others. They are generally considerate, friendly, generous, helpful, and willing to compromise their interests with others. Agreeable people also have an optimistic view of human nature. They believe people are basically honest, decent, and trustworthy.

Disagreeable individuals place self-interest above getting along with others. They are generally unconcerned with others' well-being, and are less likely to extend themselves for other people. Sometimes their skepticism about others' motives causes them to be suspicious, unfriendly, and uncooperative.

Rate yourself:

Agreeableness (friendly / compassionate vs. competitive / outspoken). A tendency to be compassionate and cooperative rather than suspicious and antagonistic toward others.

(-) Low		Rate yourself		High (+)
1	2	3	4	5

People who rate themselves high on Agreeableness usually say:

☐   People? They are infinitely interesting.

☐   I just sense others' feelings.

☐   I have a soft heart.

- ☐ I like to help people. I am usually the one that friends come to when they need a sounding board for their problems.

- ☐ I am most comfortable being around others.

Emotional Stability – Cool as a cucumber or a cat on a hot tin roof?

Emotional Stability is the tendency to experience negative emotions, such as anger, anxiety, or depression. It is sometimes called emotional instability. Those who score high in neuroticism are emotionally reactive and vulnerable to stress. They are more likely to interpret ordinary situations as threatening, and minor frustrations as hopelessly difficult. Their negative emotional reactions tend to persist for unusually long periods of time, which means they are often in a bad mood. These problems in emotional regulation can diminish the ability of a person to think clearly, make decisions, and cope effectively with stress.

At the other end of the scale, individuals who rate themselves low in emotional stability are less easily upset and are less emotionally reactive. They tend to be calm, emotionally stable, and free from persistent negative feelings.

Rate yourself:

Emotional Stability (sensitive / nervous vs. secure /confident). A tendency to experience unpleasant emotions easily, such as anger, anxiety, depression, or vulnerability.

> "Divide each difficulty into as many parts as is feasible and necessary to resolve it." – **Rene Descartes**

(-) Low		Rate yourself		High (+)
1	2	3	4	5

People who rate themselves high on Emotional Stability usually say:

☐   I am easily upset.

☐   I tend to be moody.

☐   I get irritated easily.

☐   I get stressed out easily.

☐   I sometimes feel blue.

☐   I worry about things.

Are you generally satisfied with the rankings of these traits? If not, why not?

Reflect & ReDefine™

YOUR PERSONALITY TRAITS IN THE ReDEFINITION MODEL™

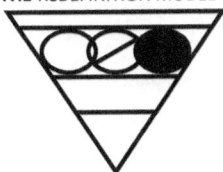

Chapter 8 Exercise
What We Should Show The World Your Personality Traits

Keep in mind that we live in the context of time thus, when we talk about redefining yourself, we're also referring to your desired future. They go hand in hand.

1. Which traits can you use to help you reach your desired future?

2. How will you leverage your present self/traits to your advantage in your desired future?

3. For each of the five traits, write an "I statement" to describe how you see yourself displaying that trait, such as, for "conscientiousness," you might say, "I love setting up my family's schedule on a huge calendar with a different color marker for each of us, with every activity and appointment laid out clearly." By doing this, you begin to see how the trait can manifest itself in your life in a real, tangible way.

PHOTO: MEDIOimages/PHOTODISC/THINKSTOCK

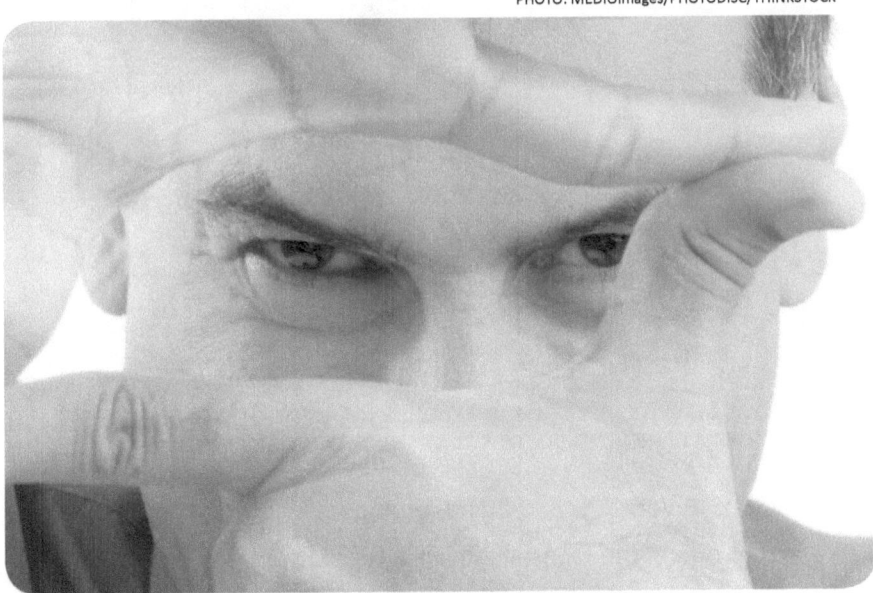

So, Where Are You Now?

Let's take a quick look back at the ReDefinition Model™. Now that you have rated yourself on the five personality traits, you have completed learning about all the "ReDefinition Drivers™." You have examined yourself based on the first two levels of the ReDefinition Model™. In the next chapter, you'll be looking at JOY, your "ReDefinition Activator™."

THE ReDefinition Model™

Copyright 2010 - McFARLAND/BRADFORD

Capture your insights about each exercise in your notebook. As you build your redefined self, all the insights work together, like puzzle pieces, to form a picture of your future. You never know what insight will connect with another one in the future to spark a breakthrough idea.

CREATIVE BREAK™

PHOTO: ANDY REYNOLDS/LIFESIZE/THINKSTOCK

Think about each personality trait as a metaphor, and use pictures (tear them from magazines and paste them on a page) to illustrate and bring each trait to life. For instance, in terms of "extroversion," are you a bright, showy peacock or a chicken that just blends into the flock? Or is "life a three-ring circus with you as the ring master?" To take this one step further, write a description of how you feel in each situation using highly descriptive language.

Think about how you would experience each trait through your five senses. Doing this helps you "try it on for size" and get comfortable or even realize that you want to adjust the rating.

Remember to capture your thoughts about the exercise in your notebook.

> "If you don't know where you are going, any road will get you there!" – **from *Alice in Wonderland***

Remember!!!

As you travel through your redefinition process, you need to remind yourself of your goals, in small but tangible ways, each day.

One way that you can remember is to create passwords for your accounts that reflect your goals. For example:

Yurf2day = Yes, you are fantastic today

Icrr2mgN = I can really reach to(2) my goals Now!

Tbiy2c! – The best is yet to(2) come !

PHOTO: PHOTO OBJECTS.NET/THINKSTOCK

"JOY" is just ahead...

PHOTO: DIGITAL VISION/THINKSTOCK

CREATIVE BREAK™

Resilience
Learning to Bounce Back
Just One More Time

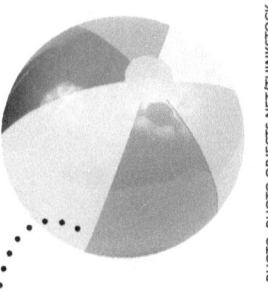

"If you get up one more time than you fall you will make it through." – **Chinese Proverb**

I heard you...you are thinking, "Sure, easy for you to say!" Consider the fact that a baby falls about 400 times before finally learning to walk. Really. You have probably already "lived" this proverb. Even if you don't feel very successful at this particular time, it is important to recognize your successes...ALL of them.

On many levels, resilience, the art of learning to fail over and over until you reach a solution is at the heart of creativity. Whether you call your "failures" prototypes, concepts or "trying just one more time," doesn't really matter. What DOES matter is continuing to examine your attempts, extract what was working and keep adding to what works until you reach a complete solution. Embrace a mindset of "one more time" and you just might discover what it really feels like to experience another great feeling – the exhilaration of a "breakthrough"!

Consider the positive impact of "recycling" on our world. The prefix "re" means to "do again, as if doing something for the very first time." As you assess your life by going through the ReDefinition Model™, you are learning to recycle your present self, your needs, core beliefs and values, and personality traits to create new direction for your life.

Try creating a list of words that begin with "re." Here are a few to get you started.

Resilience	**Re**_____	**Re**_____
Renew	**Re**_____	**Re**_____
Recharge	**Re**_____	**Re**_____

Chapter 9
The Joy of It All

PHOTO: GOODSHOT/THINKSTOCK

"Joy is not in things;
it is in us."
– Richard Wagner

In creating this ReDefinition Model™, we asked ourselves what one thing would "flip the switch" to activate the work spent examining our needs, values, beliefs, and personal traits. The answer is "joy."

So, how does joy fit into this redefinition process? Why is it even a part of our model? For so many of us, life can be joyless – we can get easily caught up in the negative. According to Dr. Rick Henson, neuropsychologist and author, there are four factors that contribute to this phenomenon called joy.

First, has to do with how our brains have been genetically programmed. Our ancient ancestors had to pay a lot of attention to negative experiences since those experiences signaled threats to their very survival. This attention to negativity has been passed down to us in our present day. The brain is wired to look for the negative. Is that really a surprise? Let's say someone gives us feedback like this: "You're doing a great job and I don't know what I'd do without you. Just remember to dot those i's." Our minds are more likely pick up on "dot those i's" and ignore the praise. Not only do certain parts of our brain store this information, it's programmed to hold on and never let go!

Secondly, although we do notice positive experiences and remember them, our brain is more sensitive to what's a threat to its survival – nowadays that would be any perceived threat to the ego; that is, any factor that tends to diminish the opinion we hold of ourselves. Take the example above – if we see ourselves as extremely conscientious, feedback about "dot those i's" would be a blow to our self-esteem. Chances are, we would dwell on that and defend ourselves in our own mind. It goes without saying that people with lower self-esteem are more vulnerable to ego threats.

Thirdly, negative experiences outweigh positive ones. Think of how one bad airline flight sticks with us more than hundreds of uneventful ones. Or if we had a meal that ended up in a food poisoning episode, we would not be likely to eat that food again no matter how many times we had consumed it prior to that one incident.

And the final contributor is our own personal training in the negative — whatever that's been. We may have grown up with critical or judging parents or maybe we lean toward "the glass is half empty" thinking. These experiences influence our view of the world and our approach to life. (Keep in mind that our personal training plays a significant role, whether our core beliefs are positive or negative.)

But wait, there is good news! After all, we are getting to the "joy" part. We can help emphasize and store positive experiences through conscious attention — intentional living. As our experience changes, our brain actually changes. It changes both temporarily and in more lasting ways. Researchers have found that different mental activities change brainwave patterns. For example, mediators have more serotonin than non-mediators; pianists have thicker brains in the areas of fine motor function. Imagine transforming a "mental rut" into a "new groove" as you refocus your attention toward your redefined self.

If we are going to shift our perspectives and discard ineffective patterns of thought and behaviors, we need to train ourselves to be more joyful.

Make Room For More Joy

Seek to be more intentional. Set a goal each day to create at least one positive, joyful experience for yourself – actively look for beauty in your world or signs of caring for you by others, or good qualities within yourself, etc.

Make a conscious decision to allow yourself to feel pleasure and be happy, rather than feeling guilty about enjoying life. Let go of any resistance for feeling good about yourself.

Listen! Just listen. Turn off the iPod, TV, computer, cell, etc.

Plan for joy. What are some activities that feel joyful to you? Use your journal to list them. Be prepared for the times when your schedule unexpectedly opens up and you have a few hours to yourself.

Give yourself the opportunity to experience new things – music, art, food, etc. Inspiration for your life can come from many different places. Think about artists. Go to art openings and experience the different types of art that is being created. Ask the artist what inspired them to chose their particular medium or subject.

Make joy a habit!

Passion and Happiness vs. Joy

Passion is about meeting our highest need. It is *outwardly* driven. Let's say our highest need is love and belonging. Helping others or being involved in a community project might be a passionate pursuit. Or let's say our highest need is power – we might be passionate about learning. Passionate pursuits need to be constantly fueled. Joy is less complicated – it comes from *within*.

Happiness vs. Joy

Some people think that happiness and joy are the same but they are not at all. Neither is better than the other. Basically, happiness generally depends on *outside* circumstances – having a baby, buying a new car or getting a new job or promotion – all these are external events that can bring us happiness depending upon what we want and expect. Joy is simple and does not depend on outside circumstances – it is based on a conscious awareness of experience. Being fully present when with a loved one, being absorbed in music, art, nature – these are the experiences of joy.

Having joy in our lives really depends upon making a conscious decision to pursue it. This is not meant to be glib. Joy is not nirvana or just for special occasions. Joyful people tend to be more stable with few extremes – neither high nor low. As scientists have learned more about the mind/body connection, joy seems to be a common denominator in the lives of those who are healthy, both emotionally and physically.

Joy seems to be a deep well that helps us deal more effectively with life. And like anything that keeps us going, we need to keep it going with a conscious effort to recharge and refill our resources. In this way, joy is similar to creativity. The more we experience joy or are creative, the more active they become in our daily lives.

"Allow yourself to trust joy and embrace it. You will find you dance with everything." – **Ralph Waldo Emerson**

Back to joy and redefinition – we believe that joy is the heart of the model – it's what drives it. A redefined self without joy is highly likely to regress back to the "old" self. Whatever we decide to do with our redefined self, our thoughts, actions and choices have to be infused with joy. Joy gives our needs, values, beliefs, and personal traits the "juice" for a vibrant future. In redefinition, if there is only one thing we change, it should be the joy factor.

Personal Training in the Joy of Living – Awakening the Joy Within

We called joy an "activator." As we move to redefine ourselves in the areas of work, relationships, and our own selves and create our desired future, sustaining the joy within is what will keep us motivated and energized. No matter what challenges we face during the redefinition process, it will be our joy that will keep our feet moving. At the same time, we will be better able to live in the present rather than living for the next moment – the next accomplishment – the next relationship.

If we don't live joyfully (intentionally), then the transition we are dealing with will easily become a regression of what once was – consequently, we live our lives without realizing much meaning or fulfillment.

As we seek to meet our needs, live according to our core values and beliefs and connect with our strengths, it is through joy that we live more purposefully. No matter what we choose to DO, what matters is HOW we do it – intentionally or not.

> "All children are artists. The problem is how to remain an artist once he grows up." – **Pablo Picasso**

Reflect& ReDefine™

YOUR JOY IN
THE ReDEFINITION MODEL™

Chapter 9 Exercise
Your Joy

Identify five of the happiest moments of your life.

Identify five joyful moments in your life.

How are they different? How are they similar?

Can you identify two activities that would increase your joy?

What are the challenges you face in consciously experiencing joy?

Think back to your earliest life. What joy did you experience then? How can you recapture that joy today?

Knowing yourself as well as you do, how can you maintain joy in your redefined self?

PHOTO: JUPITER IMAGES/BRAND X PICTURES/THINKSTOCK

CREATIVE BREAK™

"Life is not about finding yourself.
Life is about creating yourself."

— George Bernard Shaw

Like a plant, you need certain things to survive, grow and thrive. Plants need sunshine to stimulate photosynthesis and you need joy to "activate" your redefinition. Be sure that you give yourself joy each day. To create a stockpile of joy, try this exercise.

Make a list, one entry for each letter of the alphabet, of things or activities that give you joy. Keep it simple so that you will have fewer excuses not to take action. For example:

A = **A**ct silly with my (child, grandchild, etc.), ask my best friend to have coffee, etc.

B = **B**allroom dancing, balloons, blowing bubbles, etc.

Keep your list handy to choose one joyful act each day.

Getting Past Stumbling Blocks and Barriers

As you continue to redefine yourself and take steps to put your plan into action, you may experience times when thoughts just seem illusive – ideas don't flow or words are difficult to get down on paper. Don't worry! Everyone, especially when working on new ideas and habits, encounters blocks. Here are a few of the typical blocks that can occur and some things to think about if they come your way.

PHOTO: COMSTOCK/THINKSTOCK

Blocks can take the form of:

- Old habits – "Old...?" Enough said!

- Rules or rigidity – Whose rules? Let it go!

- Linear thinking – Take a detour. Zig instead of zag!

Moving past blocks...

- Take a deep breath and step back to get a different perspective.

- Switch to a new tool like writing with a pencil instead of a pen or write with your non-dominant hand.

- Turn your thinking around. If you are struggling to think of something that is fun to do, think of something that would not be fun. Then turn those thoughts back to what would be fun.

- What kind of tactics will you use the next time you encounter a block?

Chapter 10

Putting It All Together

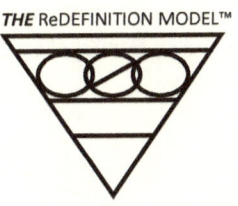

THE ReDEFINITION MODEL™

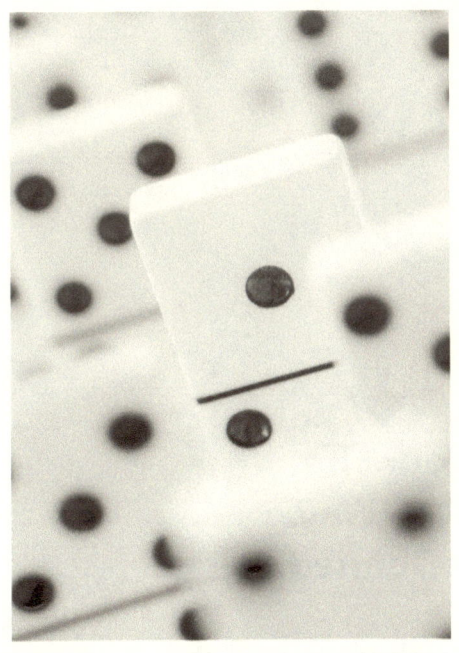

"True life is lived when tiny changes occur."
– Leo Tolstoy

You've Arrived!

All of the work you've done thus far is to be used for your final redefinition. Thus, you will need your notebook or notes to refer to as we go through this chapter.

There are three steps remaining to complete the final picture of your ReDefiniton Model™.

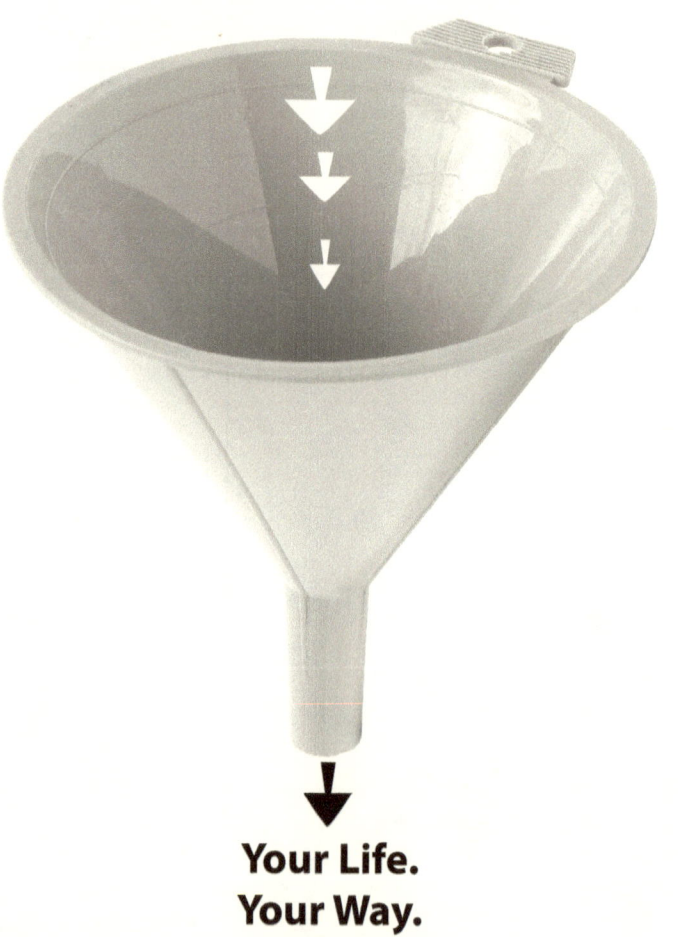

**Your Life.
Your Way.
ReDefined.™**

Step 1

Fill in the ReDEFINITION MODEL™ with *your* answers.

Look back at your notes from each of the chapters for your responses to each section of the model.

The Present Self – Chapter 5
> What I believe to be true about myself as a person.

Needs – Chapter 6
> My strongest needs and the most constructive ways to get them met.

Values – Chapter 7
> My core values and how I will live them.

Beliefs – Chapter 7
> My core beliefs and how they will influence my expectations.

Personality Traits – Chapter 8
> My personal traits and the foundation they provide for my behavior.

Joys – Chapter 9
> My joyful experiences and how I will consistently increase them.

In order to systematically record your responses, download a blank ReDefinition Model™ form at www.redefinemyself.com

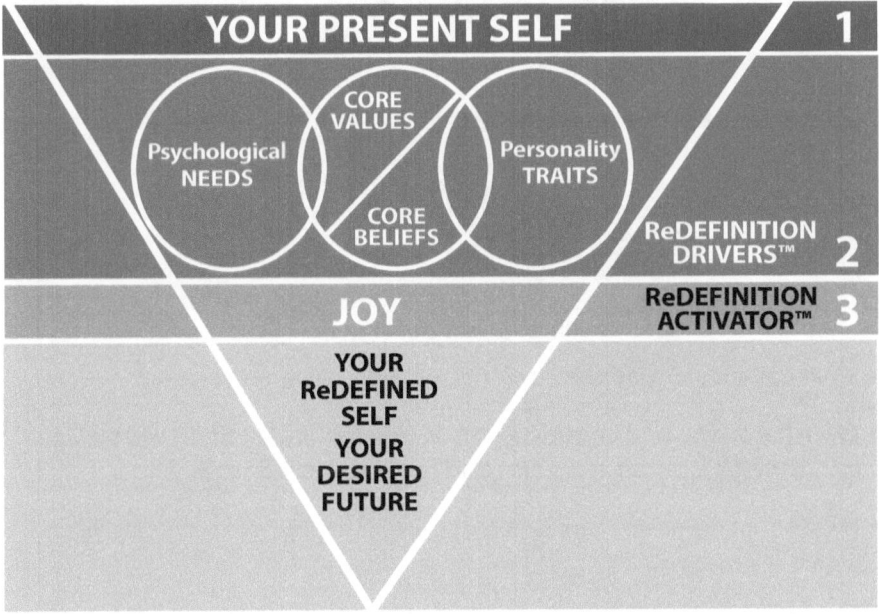

COPYRIGHT 2010 - McFARLAND / BRADFORD

Step 2

Taking into account your personalized ReDefinition Model™, answer the following "Miracle Question":

Let's suppose that tonight, you go home and go to bed as usual, but on this night while you are sleeping, a miracle happens. The miracle is that life is exactly how you want it to be. When you wake up, what would be different?

Consider these questions:

- Who's there?
- Where are you?
- What are you doing?
- What are you thinking?
- Why are you doing it?

- How will you be different?
- How will others around you be different?
- What will significant others say is different about you?
- How will you be feeling?

PHOTO: STOCK BYTE/THINKSTOCK

Now, take a closer look:

- What is it about my personality traits that will ensure my success?
- Given my needs, core beliefs and values, and personality traits, what will be one of my greatest challenges in realizing my redefined self?
- What about my needs, core beliefs and values, and personality traits will ensure my success?
- What role does joy play in my redefined self?

100

Step 3

Your Redefinition Plan Step By Step

Make your redefinition actionable. Take an aspect of your redefined self and develop an ACTION PLAN using S.M.A.R.T. Goals.

As you progress through your plan, you can create new plans for each aspect.

S.M.A.R.T. Goals help you to start living your redefinition plan.

Use the form on page 103 to work on your goals or download a larger form from our website.

S.M.A.R.T. Goals are defined as:

> **Small** – Break down larger goals into smaller steps to keep yourself moving.
>
> **Measurable** – Know what success looks like.
>
> **Achievable** – Set a goal that is within your reach.
>
> **Realistic** – Look at how each goal supports your overall redefinition plan.
>
> **Time-Sensitive** – Give yourself a specific time to complete each goal and include checkpoints to help maintain your focus and momentum.

Answer this question: How will you know that you have accomplished your goal?

_____

_____

_____

_____

_____

Take action and get busy executing your S.M.A.R.T. Goals!

Set aside a regular time on your schedule to focus on your plan. This time should be used to set, work on, and review goals and progress.

Download the ReDefinition Model™, Action Plan and S.M.A.R.T. Goals forms at www.redefinemyself.com

> "For every failure, there's an alternative course of action. You just have to find it. When you come to a roadblock, take a detour." **– Mary Kay Ash**

MY REDEFINITION ACTION PLAN

Date:
List between one and three goals along with action steps, timeframes and measures.

	GOALS What do I want to accomplish?	ACTION STEPS What do I want to accomplish?	TARGET DATES TO COMPLETE What do I want to accomplish?	MEASURES What do I want to accomplish?
GOAL #1				
GOAL #2				
GOAL #3				

RE: Momentum

Keeping your redefinition on track is a big part of reaching your goal. Look at the word "momentum." It contains the word "moment." Your redefinition happens in all the moments that you focus upon it. All those moments add up over time.

Are you saying to yourself, "Yeah, but how long can I keep this going?" You are probably like most people who have tried to start new habits that never quite took hold. The key is to make tiny changes. Chunk it down. Take it moment by moment. Help yourself build up small successes into big victories.

Focus on change in one area of your life at a time. Small changes! When you can see progress, you may be encouraged to continue.

Let's say, you're focusing on better organization in your office. Set a timer for 10 or 15 minutes and start on one corner, even one corner of your desk. If you feel like continuing after the timer goes off, keep going.

PHOTO: JUPITER IMAGES/PHOTOS.COM/THINKSTOCK

For inspiration, look at words that contain "re." As a prefix one meaning is "again" or "anew." Embrace ideas for your redefinition as an exciting process of living your life anew.

✓**Recharge**

✓**Renew**

✓**Rejuvenate**

Create a mantra for yourself. You can think of it as a tagline for your life. Look in the dictionary for other words starting with "re" if you need inspiration.

Starting to Live YOUR ReDefinition Model™

As you move toward your redefined self, it is important for you to periodically take the time to step back and see how each part is fitting together. Don't worry about perfection. Allow yourself to look at the big picture. Realize that your redefinition is malleable. The creative process is about seeing new combinations, making new connections, and giving room for things to happen.

Designers go through hundreds, sometimes thousands of different options before arriving at just the right solution – reaching that ultimate moment of "inspiration!" Speaking at a conference, James Dyson, the inventor of the Dyson Vacuum, talked about the more than 5,000 prototypes he built before putting his first vacuum on the market. Even then, he continued to make improvements and variations.

With change as the only constant in our world, we are all "works in progress." Let yourself enjoy the possibilities. What could be more exhilarating or more exciting than truly experiencing your own moments of inspiration as you begin to become your redefined self?

Remember to periodically visit our website for updates and inspiration. **www.redefinemyself.com**

Your Elevator Speech

If you have ever been asked, "So what do you do?" you needed an "elevator speech"! An elevator speech is a pithy, persuasive description of who you are. It's typically delivered within the span of time that it takes for an elevator ride – 30 seconds to 2 minutes. Those in the marketing, branding or sales fields usually have an elevator speech to explain their service, product or sales pitch.

Once you complete your ReDefinition Model™, you should be able to create an elevator speech that gets your redefined self across with clear, concise language. Working on your elevator speech is a great way to judge for yourself just how well you have redefined yourself. Once you are clear on your elevator speech, try a trial run with a friend and see how it goes. Next time someone says, "Why don't you tell me about yourself?," you will be ready to amaze them with how well-defined, you truly have become!

PHOTO: HEMERA TECHNOLOGIES/ABLESTOCK.COM/THINKSTOCK

Express Your Redefined Self

- Write your life's story as a haiku. You can only use a total of 17 syllables.

- Can you write your life's story in 10 words or less?

- If your life were a meal, what would be on the menu? Would you serve dessert? Appetizers?

- How about if your life were fashion? A period of time in fashion? Would it be the 1980's, or maybe the 1880's?

- Make your story a picture book. Choose 6-12 pictures to describe your entire life or a decade of your life.

- If you are really ambitious, create a timeline of your life depicting each decade. Put experiences on top of the dateline that you are happiest about and those that you are least happy about below the dateline. What are the any similarities between the types of experiences? The differences?

- What if your life were a map? What would that look like?

PHOTO: JUPITER IMAGES/PHOTOS.COM/THINKSTOCK

References

Amen, Daniel G. and Routh, Lisa C., Healing Anxiety and Depression
http://www.cbsnews.com/stories/2005/10/10/earlyshow/health/
main930771.shtml

Christensen, Glenn L. and Olson, Jerry C., The Pennsylvania State University, Psychology & Marketing, Vol.19(6):477-502(June 2002) Published
online in Wiley InterScience (wwww.interscience.wiley.com) copyright
2002 Wiley Periodicals, Inc. – DOI: 10.1002/mar.10021

Five Factor Model. www.personalityresearch.org
J.M. Digman's Five Factor Model. www.wikipedia.com

Glasser, William. Choice Theory and the Five Basic Human Needs
http://www.associatedcontent.com/article/404351/an_overview_of_
dr_william_glassers.html?cat=38

Hansen, Rick, Seven Facts about the Brain That Incline the Mind to Joy
www.wisebrain.org

http://www.innovationtools.com/resources/brainstorming.asp

Personality traits, www.wikipedia.com

http://www.time.com/time/healthy/article/0,8599,1882127,00.html
Study: Doodling Helps You Pay Attention, McCloud, John, Thursday,
February 26, 2009

Walonick, David S., PhD., Promoting Human Creativity, http://www.
survey-software-solutions.com/walonick/creativity.htm

Meet the Authors

Barbara McFarland, EdD

Psychologist, Author and Motivational
Speaker
www.drbmcfarland.com
www.flexlifesolutions.com

Barbara represents the left-brained part
of the writing team. As a psychologist,
corporate coach, author, and motivational speaker, Dr. McFarland
is well known for developing powerful programs for all types of
organizations. From individual coaching, train the trainer, to leadership and team solutions; she has trained thousands of clinicians,
counselors and executives how to successfully manage careers
and corporations. Her consulting and training programs have developed change agents who must meet the challenges of effective
leadership, team performance, mentoring, diversity, negotiation,
and conflict management.

Barbara has written six books – *The Balanced Life (Authorhouse,
2006)*, serves as the core curriculum for a life balance program
she developed as a support to her website, www.flexlifesolutions.
com. Dr. McFarland's programs have been successfully scaled for
success from small organizations to global corporations including
Procter & Gamble, General Electric, Cinergy, The Health Alliance
of Cincinnati, Ernst & Young, and the Xavier Consulting Group
of Cincinnati, Ohio. Her FlexLife™ seminars have been delivered
throughout North America, Asia, South America and Western
Europe. Procter & Gamble was recognized as one of the top 100
companies to work for in *Working Mother* magazine. FlexLife™
is cited as one of the programs that helped it achieve this award.

She has appeared on **Oprah, The Today Show, The Diane Rehm
Show (NPR)** and PBS and many other local news and talk shows.

Alta Bradford

Alta is the right-brained contribution to the book. Alta has always been driven by an innate curiosity for how people think and how things work. In this book, Alta combines that curiosity and her understanding of creativity, branding, trends and marketplace dynamics with her studies in psychology and sociology. Alta's expertise is in defining strategic brand objectives and leading the analysis of global branding success for a plethora of Fortune 50 brands. Alta has held positions as creative director, design director, designer and qualitative research consultant.

At the heart of every project, Alta focuses on ideas and ways to uncover rich connections that lead to the biggest ideas by connecting with what people really care about in the zeitgeist. Throughout her career, she has contributed concepts to many of the world's biggest brands. She has worked on brands that touch every part of your daily life and within every life stage from infant to adult and include products like coffee, diapers, beauty, health care, and technology. She has traveled the world, listening to and talking with consumers across many cultures.

An avocation beyond work centers on how people think and create themselves through ideas. After many years of designing brand and innovation strategies based on why people buy a specific product, Alta turns her brandcentric approach toward self-improvement.

Alta studied advertising design and illustration at Art Center College of Design. It was at Art Center that she learned the powerful connection between ideas and people.

ngramcontent.com/pod-product-compliance
g Source LLC
burg PA
545290526
00004BA/1516